An Unlikely Fooligan

Pete Haynes

HEADHUNTER BOOKS
www.headhunterbooks.co.uk

First published in February 2009 by Head-Hunter Books

ISBN 978-1-906085-14-8

Head-Hunter Books
www.headhunterbooks.co.uk

Printed in Great Britain by
Athenaeum Press Limited

For Mum & in memory of Dad (Tough Alberto)

'Kagewo tsukande jittai wo nogasuna'

'Catch not at the shadow and lose the substance'

Acknowledgments

Artwork by Julian Kirk

Thanks to:

Jon Avery
John Barnes
Chris Bragoli
Jon Charles
Tomoko Ezawa
Stefano Ferrara
Martin King
Julian Kirk
Mark Wyeth

Introduction

This is an autobiographical account of the writer's experience and feelings whilst being in Japan. It is a chronicle of two trips to Japan, the first being a week or so before the World Cup in 2002 and the second trip being a year later. The story is told through the experience of the second visit with reflections of the trip a year earlier.

By looking at another culture with no agenda but just a desire to have a break, the traveller developed an awareness of his own society by comparing it to Japan. Quite unintentionally the traveller's idle musing took an informal sociological perspective. The telling is not academic but subjective with tongue firmly in cheek as feelings and observations are recounted for the reader to share and hopefully enjoy. 'Fooligan' is a mispronunciation of the word given for the English football 'hooligan'. This unlikely fooligan goes about in his own harmless way but because of his physical presentation, he incurs the attention of the indigenous people who respond to what the media have given and see him as one of the 'fooligans' that will be arriving for the World Cup. Yet this traveller is no fooligan as he seeks out pastry shops and meets people of warmth and good humour; he was welcomed by the ordinary Japanese person and even sworn in as a Girl Guide in a late night ceremony in a Kyoto bar.

In conclusion the observer casts a look at his own society and he doesn't sit on the fence in venting his feelings to the way of things.

One

So, Japan. What about it? It will take you twelve hours, if the plane doesn't crash of course, to fly direct from Heathrow airport which is on the west side of London, to Narita airport which is about thirty miles on the east side of Tokyo. I have been to Japan twice. On my first trip I flew on Japan Airlines direct to Narita and on return had a direct flight back to Heathrow. I was taken by the attitude of the people working on the plane; their politeness and manner was extremely pleasing. On my second outing, I flew with Air France which took a long time as I had a couple of planes to catch. First off, flying to Paris, taking under an hour, then at least a couple of hours waiting before a twelve and a half hour flight to Narita; I must say the staff on the Air France flights were also pleasant.

There are some principal differences in culture and specific mannerisms between Japanese people and the people in the culture from where I come from. One example is that there isn't the propensity for men to walk with their shoulders and adopt that all too well known presentation of an aggressive self that is maybe used as a defensive measure that we are all very aware of in the UK. When setting out to write this little account I didn't intend to have rambling thoughts about the history of the Japanese culture and factors that determine the behaviour of its inhabitants. There were no thoughts in my mind at all about discussing social theories. This is just my travelogue, giving the insights and feelings that I had whilst being in Japan and in no way attempting to add some kind of contribution to an analysis into the Japanese psyche. My aim was just to accept what I found in Japanese behaviour and not to get involved with the why's and wherefore's but to just look at the way it is or as I chanced upon it. Although during the end of my second trip, unexpected thoughts came to my mind when contrasting the differences between Japanese culture and that from in the West. Sorry to have gone on at such lengths to explain myself. So, here we go.

A year had passed between making the two trips and I have to say it felt just like a week or even the same week because that's what it felt like when I was ambling about on my second outing. Geisha girls, school girls, atomic bombs, a sexual fetish for hurting girls in pornography, bullet trains, sleeping capsules in hotels, polite manners, raw fish, eating fish that can fatally poison you, expensive prices, being nationalistic, unyielding hunting practices in the seas, Mount Fuji, Sumo wrestlers, chopsticks, electronic gadgets and cameras, Nissan cars, very crowded underground trains, karate and other martial arts, karaoke, groups of Japanese tourists taking photographs as one in an obsessive flurry, cartoon magazines, sake, kimonos, cherry blossom, short people, hara kiri, Samurai warriors and all their swords and stuff, game shows, kamikaze pilots – cruelty. These are a few of the wonderful things. These are popular images and misconceptions or ideas about the place and the people and are as common to me as they are to you. They are generalised notions that people have about 'the land of the rising sun' or TLOTRS.

I went there because I was told it was 'different'. I was told it was a place, although having problems like any other place, where a person can wander around and be left unhindered. I was told it was safe in terms of robbers and violence and free from the thug mentality that has more than ruined the country from where I come from. I was getting depressed and anxious as I took a long and negative overview of the society that I lived in from the slimy top dogs, fat cats or whatever name has been given to them and all the scheming, greedy, spineless and bullying nasty types that range from politicians, company big wigs, those in the social and legal professions who earn a living out of their product – to the cowardly thugs and pathological social retards that you and I are unlucky enough to come across on an everyday basis.

I was told by a person whom I know that in Japan I could go drinking at anytime and there would be no problem, no random beating from a passing bunch of youngsters demonstrating that they are nothing but a waste of space. It is different I was told. It is a place where you can relax and, if you are so inclined, take pleasure in experiencing that difference. As I said before, I didn't go to Japan with any ideas of trying to understand the reasons why it is different.

And that is what I did. I went and stayed at a friend's place in the suburbs of Tokyo. He has lived there for years and is married to a Japanese woman. This chap has known me for a long time and when he visited Blighty to see his mum the previous Christmas, I was telling him in good neurotic fashion about how the state of our society was filling me with constant apprehension and that there did not seem any respite from the malice syndrome that I felt pervaded the island where we live. At that time I was locked in a bracket where my thinking circled around thoughts that the honest men and women pay through the nose and more for everything that they have and they're getting short changed; the innocent and vulnerable were being attacked from many angles. And I felt and still do, that there is a culture developing where there is becoming fewer places of sanctuary from the mainstream for people who might not fit in with the general flow. I vented my feelings as I ranted to my friend that these people aren't criminals. They have a code of ethics, knowing right from wrong in the honest sense but because they don't conform fully to the fickle demands that might be in fashion, they aren't accommodated and are often derided. Those who do not pitch their voice to the consensual tone have their voices muted and are often alienated as a negative type by some in the media along with those occupying positions of authority in the public services, the literary world and the arts. For this seems to be the process of censorship and those having the power to do so will sanction selective preferences – the oppressors are in their liberal clothing having voices of neutrality but carrying out actions that are decidedly partial for their own interests.

And when one goes to the most picturesque village, there exists an exhibition of aggressive behaviour and often malevolent attitudes that are expressed by the young and old, female and male, in different ways but being the actions of resentment – and I for one was generating a powerful state of paranoia. The craven and hypocritical attitude of allowing the thug mentality and the more educated thugs to target the honest and fragile was getting

me down to a point where I was going to do something! But what?
Well....

My friend told me to go to a place and unwind, to go somewhere different. He understood what I meant and told me that indeed those were some of the reasons why other people wanted to get away and had flown over half way around the world to do so. He told me to just take his word for it. He said he would arrange a little itinerary for me organising things like staying in a Japanese hotel, participate in having a Japanese bath and visit places of interest. He has a great knowledge of Japan. Having lived there for years, he speaks the language fluently and of course is married to a Japanese woman. My friend knows that I am what some would call a bit of an individual so I could use his place as a base and do my musing and mooching about at my free will.

I booked the time off from my job and flew off. He was right. Although it gets a bit trying making yourself understood and of course there are the differences that can and do nark if one was to be there for a long time but, that being said, I felt it was the best place I had been. For me, it was just the friendliness of the people. By being friendly I mean not threatening I suppose because I was left to wander at will without fear.

And even if the friendliness was superficial as some people will say it is, it didn't bother me. My purpose was to get lost in a different feel and to do it in a country where people have a decent standard of living and value themselves. I couldn't go to one of those places where begging is an industry and I don't mean London. I'm talking about places where children make for an early grave because of the abject poverty that they were unlucky enough to be born into. I would feel like an arrogant intruder utilising the people and place without honest respect. I have never thought of going to many of the places that the normal traveller might consider interesting. I would find it embarrassing and wouldn't be surprised at all if the people who live there hated and bore me a grudge. I would understand it if they wanted to rob me because of the economic twiddling that has caused them to be seen as little more than appendages in the playground life experienced by many students from the prosperous parts of the world who gaze at, examine and learn about during a gap year or holiday. Sometimes I feel it's not much different from going to a zoo; there is a distance.

No, that's not for me. I like the idea of being in a place where the inhabitants are their own people and don't have to bow and scrape to some idiot who tries to dress like one of the indigenous population in a scheduled break from their career. Anyway, I don't wish to labour the point. I just wanted to walk unnoticed but of course one will be noticed by the obvious differences. I didn't want to be beholden to anything. I wanted to just be and meander aside from the normal daily way of life.

It was a good feeling, being an alien and conversely I felt accepted because of my alien status rather than at home where one can feel different because of the feeling of being alien. It felt comfortable. Being separate in a foreign land, the heat is taken out of social situations. There is no self-doubt as one is obviously different and therefore not part of everything or anything. There is no competition, no judgement from the domestic people. It's a pleasant experience when feeling safe and being an outsider in another culture. I noted the feelings that I had and the observations I had made but not in a book, only in my mind and it wasn't in a conscious way to speculate or have an opinion. That would happen quite subconsciously during my second trip. I noticed things like the use of different colours as a culturally pleasing aesthetic, the way they are used in advertising, such as the pale colours of pinks and yellows. It had a lighter feel, neon blazes from buildings and there is an abundance of streamers decorating the windows of stores. Everything seemed at a higher pitch, maybe accordant with a significant cultural tone. It was evident everywhere - in the voices, music and physical movements. After all this is a different land.

At the end of my first trip, I felt that it was what I needed and I liked it. I was a bit bored with my own company at times but that's the way it is. It was a good trip as they say. On the last day of my trip I arrived at the airport to catch my plane but found that I had come a day late ! The plane I was meant to catch had left the day before although, dear reader, it all ended up well as it was resolved in a manner that left me liking Japan more and more. But, dear reader of this little jaunt of mine, it was during this episode of confusion at the airport when I was in a situation where there could have been an altercation - but confrontation isn't the way of things in Japan - that I was given an insight or saw a chink in the bridled armour that defends this island people. And that, dear reader, changed everything – not exactly turning the feeling to swing from 'sweet' to 'sinister' but all the same, well stick with me and you'll see what I mean.

What happened was this. I stayed in a hotel near the airport the night before coming home so I didn't have to rush the morning of my return flight. Being extremely nervous of flying I thought I would minimise anxiety by cutting out factors that can contribute to tension, stress and all of that. So, by staying at a hotel near the airport meant that I didn't have to travel across Tokyo in the morning to catch my flight because forty odd miles of changing trains in teeming, swarming conditions would be stressful and things would be further compounded by not knowing what train to get and what platform it would be leaving from if I did find out what train to catch and by the way, platforms are referred to as 'tracks' in Japan. And of course, throw into the mix the matter of language difficulties and the risk of being late and then having to rush - no - I booked a room in a hotel near to the airport, went for a beer in a local bar and reflected on what was a very pleasant trip.

I went to the airport in the morning. It was all going to plan - what could go wrong? I was only five miles away from the airport and I had checked out how to get there the previous day. So I arrived there with time to spare wearing an inane grin caused by dread, a presentation of a genial foreigner - but when checking in it was pointed out to me by a young women that my flight had in fact left the day before. Yes - oh yes it was. She pointed to the date on the ticket and then continued to question me about turning up a

day late. Her face was young and soft and it was turning from corporate friendliness to serious concern. Her expression showed incredulousness that a person could make such a mistake. I explained that I am nervous about flying and that, maybe, even subconsciously, I had turned up a day late because of my massive fear of it all. This didn't translate so I bumbled embarrassed and anxious apologies for my stupidity. She told me to wait where I was whilst she went off and spoke to somebody. She returned with another young woman who looked at me momentarily. I felt as if she was assessing me before speaking. Through her politeness and ready to serve deportment, there was a driving efficiency adhering to rules and behaviour. She questioned me. "Why? Why was I a day late? Why?" Over and over she asked me and my reply was the same as I had given to the other young woman. They both stood and looked at me, their look of scrutiny gaining intensity and again the same question with increasing perplexity at my behaviour. "But why?" The second one went off after telling me quite curtly to remain where I was. I looked at the young woman who was standing with me. She watched me with curiosity. I offered a weak smile. I was prepared to pay the fare. I had accepted this as the cold reality of the situation. It would be a shame but it wouldn't blight a good trip – and that's the way it goes. Other passengers looked at me. The Japanese ones knew what had happened by hearing the two young women talking and saying God knows what about me. I relaxed for I had accepted my fate.

Then number two returned and again the question. "Why?" She pointed to the date on the ticket for the umpteenth time and looked at me, her eyes altered contour as she tried to fathom me and I looked into her young face, a face and body that was petite and slender, wearing a uniform that showed an undercurrent of strength and authority residing beneath her elegant presentation – and then she turned to her colleague and off she went again. And I waited. And waited and then she returned but something strange happened. I had a feeling just before she came up to me that it would be all right. I felt a glimmer of hope, even bordering on the confident side of it all that things were going to work out. I thought that I would be let off as they came to understand that I wasn't lying or being deceitful. I wasn't mocking or making a fool of the system. I felt that they dealt in a currency that was honesty. I was being honest. A thought came to me that if I was attempting to pull the wool over their eyes they would come down heavily but as I was being genuine it might, hopefully, be accepted. On the one hand they couldn't understand such crass stupidity for getting something wrong like going to the airport on the correct day, yet on the other hand I wasn't trying to cheat the order and was acting in an honourable way, even by showing myself as half-witted and lacking.

I felt that I had seen through their polite shield. At first it was just a sliver of light but it quickly became a gaping chasm in which I saw the internal nature or spirit of the Japanese order of things where there is an observation to the rules and having confusion towards misbehaviour if it was not functional. The cross questioning that they gave me reminded me of playing war games at primary school when aping German SS officers, firing questions in a short and stark manner. The stereotypical response played out by children at that time as determined by images that came from the media. Here, the two young women seemed to be exhibiting that same blind faith to a regime. It appears obscure for them when conjuring with the concept of the individual for it is seen as inconsequential because it is the mass that is important and having concerns for striving to manifest company and State objectives. Maybe I saw an element to all of this during our tense interaction. I wasn't representing rogue behaviour. I was just simple and the State is seen to understand those who just slip and are not out to challenge or counter the rule. It made everything feel different. The young woman walked up to me and her manner was softer and she gave me back my useless ticket and said without any waver in her voice that was set in a pleasing smile. "Please accept apologies of Japan Airways for delaying you. There is no charge. Please accept flight on Japan Airways."

I looked at her and then I looked at the other girl. Her gaze was also unrelenting, both relieved that they had performed a function. I spluttered my gratitude, wanting to kiss and hug her. And so I got on the plane for Blighty. But, through all of that, it felt a little spooky. I got onto the plane thinking these are the best people that I have come across. It seemed honest, harsh but honest and I pondered that there was nowhere on planet Earth that has a great amount of people living together in what is commonly referred to as a society that is good in all ways but for someone like me, well, I felt that I could cope with an authoritarian State with its, supposedly, robotically propelled people if the outcome was to be left in peace when going about one's business.

The friendliness and accommodating nature carried on during the flight when I asked a stewardess if there might be some little memento for my nephew who was aeroplane mad. A bloke in one of the other seats translated it and she came back with a copy of what I believe is called 'the course of flight' that had information on weight, cargo, the places the plane flew over and all that. The captain signed it, it was nice, it was amiable and I liked it. It was simple but then I am simple. It was enough. It was what I wanted. And we all flew safely home.

Two

And so, a year later I made a return trip. Why? Well, I had the time and money to do so and also there remained a desire to get away from things at home for a while. Nihon was familiar and I knew a couple of people with whom I could stay but there was something else, something I couldn't put my finger on. I just wanted to go and have another look at Japan, its people and ways. I intended to travel around on the bullet train and stay in a few different places. I had two contacts in Japan. One was my friend Chris in Isehara who I stayed with the previous year and the other was Jon who was living in the centre of Tokyo. He is a city dealer type who was away from Tokyo on work when I visited the year before but this year he was at his flat. He told me to get hold of him and that I was welcome to stay. So I gave both of them a ring, booked a flight and bought the special rail pass that allows extensive travel on Japan Railways that included the standard bullet train. It's a rail pass that can only be booked outside of Japan and by non-Japanese nationals. I then bought new underpants, socks and some bits and pieces and I was ready to go. With my bag packed I flew to TLOTRS with an open mind. In fact, a blank mind and on landing, a mind that was just relieved that the flight went okay. White concrete. This was what I thought on my first trip. The place reminded me of an American Air Base having the same coloured grey and flat coloured steel and metal. For $ome reason the roads reminded me of the United States but I didn't know what it was but I would later know why.

As on my first trip I headed for Isehara, taking a bus from Narita that went to Tokyo and then down to Yokohama which is south of the big city before moving westwards through the suburbs for another thirty miles. On our journey through Tokyo, a developing Disney Land was pointed out to me. I looked at some of the absurdly affected buildings. The fabricated constructions with the sugar puff dusting is a creation denoting that other world of fantasy having its spiritual base somewhere in Florida or California and now they were transferring that fantasy into a rain sodden Tokyo pollution. It was being erected in a poisonous and infecting haze, lying beneath a dark and heavy cloud cover that hid from the rushing commuters a sky that was blue and set high. The illusory paradise that is presented as a never, never world of sunshine escapism was at this moment a far off notion as we passed the twisted metal and concrete frenzy that looked like a painful operation imposed in a saturated carbon monoxide ridden quagmire that was already overly cramped for breath. Wiping the mist from the window of the bus, I turned in my seat and, with the tiredness of travelling, I thought about the great American imagination making pre-emptive plans for their theme park in the event of an earthquake. But it would be Disney style, a designer earthquake theme, not open until the real earth ripper makes its appearance.

I felt tired. It was that nervous tiredness. I watched the back of the bus driver's head, catching a glimpse of the peak on his hat when he turned to check the wing mirror and I looked at the driver's profile. I don't know why but noticing the shape of his nose and chin. Looking out of the window, I contemplated the people in the cars, vans and lorries. All of them were Japanese or looked Japanese to me. I looked around myself and thought, "I am here again, my second journey". It felt different from before. People have different reasons for wanting to travel. It might be to have a break from the familiarity of one's own country or to escape from one's routine and some do their travelling to a structured plan. Others might be looking for something and maybe not knowing what it was and there are those who know exactly why they are going. The reasons could be for sport, history, sun, pursuing their hobby, sex or whatever. On that first trip, mine was to escape from a culture that was getting me down with its cowardice, bullying and aggressive behaviour and go to a country where a person does not have to look over his or her shoulder and always be wary of an imminent physical threat from people in various situations whether that be walking alone at night in a built up or quiet area, waiting for a taxi late at night or seeing a group of blokes and expecting to be glared at or insulted or even being beaten and robbed or worse.

I was told that there is a place on Earth where it isn't like that and it was true. I had gone there myself and seen it, albeit only for a couple of weeks. I was told of the frustration and coercion that exists just beneath the surface but as I said before this wasn't in my mind to find out why, only my personal being and experience was the concern but that was on my first visit. Although not conscious when wanting to return to Nihon, I would be taking a closer look at the place and its people and that is what happened – dear reader of this little travelogue.

So, now I had come back. My mind was a little more tranquil than it was on my previous visit when my reason for going there was for a metaphorical good clean, wash and bath if you like but now, with that being done, I was looking around the bathroom where I had enjoyed my ablutions. A ridiculous metaphor indeed. I was interested in having a look at the people and the place but this time with a less crowded mind. I was going to have a clearer gaze with a more staid mind. I had also set myself a little quest. Nothing life changing or seeking the esoteric. No. I know it sounds quirky but it was in the back of my mind to keep an eye out for any overtly boisterously macho type of behaviour. Why? I don't know. It was little more than something to amuse me because I had considered such a presentation of conduct as being out of place in Japan. It was also perverse wit when I considered that my main reason to get away from Blighty was to go somewhere to escape from aggressive people. There must have been some morbid, post-traumatic, subliminal counter fear exploration in my little fancy. I don't know. Some neurotic tinkering at play I suppose. Yet, it struck me as amusing to think that in this ordered polite society, there might be in a parallel existence, that is, the Japanese version of the shoulder bowling, hostile staring, strutting 'geezer' who is found everywhere in the UK. It would have been difficult to talk about this at a counter in a tourist board office, trying to explain to the person on the other side of the desk about the image and ways of a geezer and the possibilities of tracking down the equivalent in Japan.

In all honesty I knew that there wouldn't be the geezer because he is a creation from a different cultural mix from that which exists in Japan and, of course, it was just a whimsical joke to humour myself with. All the same, I would keep a casual eye out to see if there was an exhibition of geezer behaviour.

Now I wish to make myself clearly understood here. What I mean is the friendly everyday geezer behaviour. A chap having a pleasant manner even if seen as being a bit rough around the edges. Yet, of course, there is also a geezer presentation of behaviour demonstrated by many that veers towards the macho type having the masculine manner that is believed by the actors who adopt this presentation of self as epitomising a psyche and language held by tough men. I believe that it germinates from inner repression, a psychological cavern where deference exists. Indeed and servility towards those that they fear and see as one's betters. It is a classical British class structure dictate where the working class man, the manual worker, has a different body language from men who work in offices say. This is proper man's world where one can observe the geezer behaviour of holding his cigarette inwards to the palm of the hand, walking with toes pointed outwards, wearing a capped sleeved tee shirt when the temperature is minus ten, growling blunt demands and replies in shops, having rings that are really euphemisms for knuckle dusters, making a big show by extending their arm when letting someone exit or enter a doorway, standing with arms folded and nodding gravely at the person they are talking to with legs splayed so wide apart it looks if he is making room for a small car to pass through them, to scratch and rearrange his bollocks every seven seconds, shout over people and affect a rasping, gravely throaty effect in speech, take a dog out for a walk as if it's a threat. This is the classic geezer behaviour and all that goes with it wouldn't exist if the social determinates weren't in place that produces that mentality. I believe that the aggressive personality rests on feelings of inferiority and resentment coming from an oppressed soul.

What does it say about the land that I come from?

But, all that said, my anthropological pursuit was just a silly survey for the geezer ways and not to find nasty violent thugs because that's not what I mean at all. They are around everywhere. No, it was a search for those characteristics that are in a way cartoon like and making a travesty of human adulthood. It was only a harmless musing, nothing serious. Just my own silly little search. Maybe it had something to do with having too much time on my hands or an idle mind. I don't know. Simple mind might be more accurate. Yes, simple. I was going to a place and had the opportunity to gain an insight into the country and meet some of the people and also keep an eye out for a geezer. It would be an interest and something to pursue on my travels, something to fall back on I suppose when things went a bit flat and boring. Just as there are those who have their interests and wish to pursue them when travelling, albeit more orthodox, such as angling, photography, mountaineering or whatever it may be. I was out to bump into people who aren't met in the typical tourist grooves. It would be those Japanese people that are not normally met by the outsiders.

An Unlikely Fooligan

Now, an outsider is what non-Japanese people are commonly referred to in Japan. By outsider, I mean the non-Japanese people working and living in Japan. They are people who have lived in Japan for many years, living there because of work or wanting to get away from their home country. They are the gap year teachers and the ones that stayed and the business people who in the main revolve in a bubble of a Western corporate culture. And because of this, they never really get to know and experience the life of the normal indigenous person. During my first trip, I was taken to a couple of bars and a mock pub setting in Tokyo that was used by the gaijin, the Japanese word for foreigner or outsider. It wasn't what I wanted. I could have stayed in London if I wanted to meet the city and geek fraternity at play. It is often the case, I have learned, that this type of person often doesn't share the lives of ordinary people where they come from, meaning that they find it difficult or feel that it's difficult to fit in. And I travel all the way to Tokyo encounter these types, the cyberspace guys, the gimpy anorak who has now come of age, extolling ego's on the internet and often speaking in a cartoon comic character style of language coming from the United States, having a vocabulary that is marbled with a speech consisting of labels and terminology when, once remembered, associates them to a culture that they can hide behind because they seem to struggle when presenting their own imagination and identity. It's depressing to ponder that they might even despise what they really feel about themselves and are ever scared of that feeling of inadequacy residing within – just as long as they are seen as saying the right thing.

This new eclecticism of borrowing and using from a world culture has its quintessence placed firmly within the costly and designer led consumerism that is heady on consumptive yearning, having a mind-set where originality of thought and action is an impossibility when the central focus is delivering functional prerequisites that are the demands of the corporate ideals. All this whilst, ostensibly, remaining loyal to the 'going it alone' principle emanating from the rugged individualistic ideology that is the principal myth in the thinking that exists in the United States of America. A philosophy that is perpetuated in films and literature and here are the children of this monetarist mantra, the liberal elite revelling in the new world playground. I saw those who are out of kilter in the places where they come from establish themselves once in the safe territory of the 'other'. They can then recreate the stage and settings of an environment and often emulate the behaviour of the people that intimidated them 'back home' except it is more like an A grade student end of term affair where the edge and unknown doesn't exist and so the threat is eliminated. It's cosy and it's a career-led existence shared with like minded associates. These expatriate workers have their culture. It isn't one that I share and each to his own. I wasn't to follow the designer experience of ticking off items on a contrived itinerary of things to do and see. I wanted to get lost, not in geographically remote areas or to undertake a deep investigation into the sub worlds and also not to embark on a deep voyage into the soul or of gaining and learning any great handle on aspects Japanese. No. My trip was to be just a pleasant and humble saunter in my idle suburban way and graze amongst my fellow beings.

Three

I stayed in the flat of my friend and his wife on the first few days of my second trip just I had done during my first trip. Jet lag affects some more than others. It hits me like a steel door slamming into my body. The effect is similar to some of the symptoms of having flu. I don't drink alcohol on the plane and I can't sleep in the air; the effects last for nearly a week and that's a bad thing when one is only in a place for two weeks. It gives a perception of being detached, amplifies the differences and compounds the feeling of weirdness and over sensitivity. Yes, dear reader, what a sensitive little soldier I am. For those first few days I lounged around in bed, going out to the local shops and indulged in a regular pastime of mine of hanging around a railway station. The station at Isehara is a good one being quite large and conjoined to department stores and convoluted enough in its physical construction to make it confusing for a visitor, especially with the language difference. It doesn't sound very interesting but just being away from my usual surrounding was enough for me. All I wanted was a place to relax in and have a ponder. I liked the place and although sounding mundane that's how I often gain pleasure, by watching the ordinary goings on in everyday life. I like to feel it, the sounds, colours, tastes, smells – everything, the small things and that which is usually seen as insignificant are for me often the things that embody the interesting characteristics making up what is the difference between cultures. I knew that my hosts thought my activities were a bit too banal and that it was a long way to come just to walk down the road, hang around the station, idle in shops and around the streets and in the evening have a couple of beers in a back street bar but that is what I did. It is just me.

The concrete conglomerate mass in which the bulk of people dwell on Honshu (the main island that is one of the islands making up Japan) has gathered itself around Tokyo and spreads out so far it makes the suburbs of London seem little more than a village setting or something like that. Isehara is in the suburbs of Tokyo, about thirty miles west from the centre of the city yet one doesn't have a sense of leaving Tokyo whilst travelling on the train out to Isehara because the concrete doesn't stop. There is less intensity in its construction but if one puts one's head down and walks, one will surely bump into another person in about four and a half seconds and one would say, 'gomen nasai' which according to my little Japanese phrasebook I bought, means, 'I'm sorry'. I learned that short phrase and used it all the time. I liked it and it was reciprocated or initiated by the inhabitants of the land that I was visiting as they presented their polite social manners.

There are little restaurants around the station area and one can buy a meal at a very reasonable price. Although it is common to believe in the country where I come from that everything is expensive in Japan, let me tell you that it isn't. It might have been or was years ago but during the times that I made my visits I didn't find many things that different in price. I liked the food and, when looking in the windows of the restaurants, one will often see plastic models of the different dishes with the name of whatever the dish is called next to it. It looks a precise skill and I was told that it is a big industry which is pretty obvious I suppose when one considers that eating out in Japan is a very common indulgence. I was told that it helps, what with the language difficulties, to just point at what one wants if one likes the look of a dish. It amused me but I never did bring a waiter or waitress out of the restaurant and point at the plastic representation of a certain meal. As it happens, I'm not a restaurant going type of person. I liked the little sushi packs with the hot green horseradish and tofu, especially a sweet little tofu pudding. I'm very basic with food but I liked Japanese food very much and liked the courteous manner in which it was handed over to me.

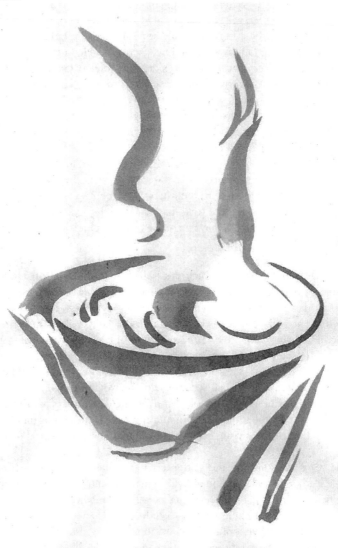

Around the station complex is a small network of crossing roads and internal walkways taking one in or out of the station area and leading into one of the department stores. I liked the fact that everyone was Japanese or looked it to me. Whilst walking around, one will hardly ever see a foreign looking face in the milling crowd. I must have stood out as my bulky frame took up more space than the average person and my pace wasn't hurried as I meandered with my languid gait. I told my friend's wife, when she asked if I thought it a bit dull to hang around the station, that the station and the area around it is an open museum. I didn't need or want to have things selected and collated by 'professionals' and exhibited in a constructed and formulated way for me to gape at because I like to make up my own mind. I believe that it is in the minute detail of everyday life that one will gain a clearer and truer insight and understanding of the bigger picture. I'm not sure how my, probably cranky, thoughts were considered by her but all the same that's what I did.

The elderly people in Japan, most of them, had lived through a life of not having the calcium and maybe protein in their diets that the generations that came after them have had. This is evident by looking at their physical size and the amount of older people showing the effects of bone deficiencies, such as bow legs; that kind of thing. Listen, I'm no medical person. It's just an observation and when I enquired about what I saw this is what I was told. I noticed that the looks I was getting from a lot of the older people wasn't what would be taught in a 'meet and greet' course run by a consultancy lecturing on corporate hospitality. Ingrained or seemingly so, into their faces is a look that reflects a dislike and maybe a suspicion of the foreigner. The look told me that they didn't want the outsider around them. I couldn't help thinking of the Second World War, of the hardship these people had faced and to have had the supremacy dream exploded in front of their eyes – and to have lost and so becoming subservient to a victorious external and different people. Their look told me that the current activities in modern Japan might be considered and accepted as normal and it is the way of things in order for the younger people to survive but and very much 'but', it looked like it was a very bitter pill for the older folk to swallow. I saw it as a look of resentment and that these older members of this country didn't and maybe couldn't, do what is the Japanese thing to do and that is to adopt a disguise to hide behind. No. They didn't wear a mask to shield their real feelings. This has been the integral essence that has allowed the Japanese to retain their autonomy in Asia through the ages. It is the way of showing acquiescence to another culture with the objective to adopt and adapt in the function of surviving but concealed beneath whatever mask is shown exists the same Japanese character and intent.

I noticed the older people everywhere, being small in physical size among the throng of people, although not looking as if they were cast aside. They were not part of the mainstream rush that sped people up and down stairs, to jostle in gatherings in doorways or to frenetically check watches with a look on their hurried faces that read work. I don't know what the official retirement age is in Japan. I had probably asked and I've forgotten if I did but I was told that, in the main, older people are respected and there are schemes in place that accommodated older people to have a function in society when they had retired from what was their job and remember that a job was for life in Japan. For many Japanese people, it is important to feel that one is part of and contributing to the great social machine and to participate daily in one of the many mechanisms making up the collective.

I saw older people working in various jobs such as telling people to stand in an orderly line on a railway platform or working as a group standing around a hole that was being dug in the road and directing people around the barrier surrounding the hole and the men who were digging it. It was pointed out to me that within the group of elderly people, there is a tier of ranking and that the person having the higher status would have had a higher status when he, it's usually a 'he', was in his regular job before retirement. Uniforms are very popular in Japan and the elderly participants aiding and supporting on the periphery of action are proud to have their uniforms. I was told there are symbols such as badges, stripes and the like denoting the person's status in the ranking. On more than one occasion I caught the eye of one these uniformed elders going about their duty. His face would harden and a command was spat out and although having no real change in facial expression, I felt there was a dislike with thoughts of me being stupid but I'm not getting carried away with feelings of being picked on for being an 'outsider'. The indigenous people also feel the sharp edge of the tongue and a wrathful glare from these senior citizens who command veneration.

There is a bus station in Isehara. It's all a bit cramped and it takes careful manoeuvring to reverse the buses back out into the street so that they can drive off to complete another route. There would be at least one of the senior workers, dressed in a uniform, standing in the street directing the intricate operation with utmost concentration. Traffic was stopped as the senior worker waved a stick that had a light on the end of it and in what I took to be deliberate series of movements, the baton was waved in a way that I thought must have had significance, like a semaphore system. When I asked about this, I was told that there wasn't such a thing and these people just made it up. All the same they performed the duty with great diligence.

One afternoon I stood and looked at the smartness of the man's uniform as he shepherded the bus, monitoring its reversal into the street, casting castigatory glares at motorists who didn't heed his instructions to full compliance. Pedestrians were also given a roasted glare and told off if ignoring instructions or simply daydreaming. As I went to walk around the back of this man, he emitted an order at me that was made by a strangulated sound forced from his throat. His eyes narrowed and contempt exuded from his being at my lack of observance to his order and also I was a foreigner. I did as I was commanded to do and nodded an apology but it was met with a lingering stare that was unforgiving before turning his attention to the main business of getting the bus on its way. It amused me. Not just to be chided in this way but the situation. It was different to what I was used to. A motorist who was waiting patiently gave me a look that said I would learn as everyone has to succumb to the ruling of these senior workers.

On another occasion, as I waited for a bus to be reversed into the street, the senior worker was giving the bus driver a particularly hard time. I don't know what it was but it seemed that the driver wasn't following the instructions being given to him as he should have done. The senior worker did indeed appear to be berating the driver in quite an aggressive manner. On noticing that I was watching what was going on, the driver turned in his seat and acknowledged me with a resigned lazy blink of his eyes. His look said, 'that is the way of things and this is my lot'.

But it wasn't only in an official capacity that I saw older people directing damning looks and telling people what to do. One of the occasions that I was reminded in matters of manners and rules happened as I entered into the covered area of the station in Isehara one rainy day. The area led off to the ticket office and platforms and in another direction leading to the entrance of a department store. I had noticed these little plastic sheaves tied together next to the doorway and had wondered what they were. On this occasion I was to find out because as I stood there with my umbrella dripping onto the concrete and tiled floor, I became aware of an old lady scolding me. At first I didn't realise what she was going on about and looked around myself but indeed it was me that she was directing her venom at. Then it became apparent what it was all about when a passing traveller pointed at my dripping umbrella and then at the little plastic sheaves that were provided and hanging by the doorway. One has to fold one's brolly and insert it into the plastic sheaf thus stopping any rain water dripping onto the surface of the floor thus making it a safer area as one wouldn't slip and thus having respect for one's immediate environment and all that it entails. A few people looked on as I nodded and offered my apologies. Some of those passing by smiled at me yet were careful that their supporting gesture wasn't noticed by the old lady whose fury hadn't lessened at all. She might not have had many teeth in her mouth and her physical bearing had shrunken and bowed but the dynamite was still ready to go in her eyes. I ambled over in a self conscious manner to the bundle of little sheaves and found it awkward to insert the umbrella in the plastic wrapping. So clumsy and stupid was I in my ungainly western way and when I looked up having performed the task, feeling that I had done the right thing and having acceded to cultural expectations, I saw that the old lady was glaring at me. The reprimanding look hadn't cooled one degree and she muttered something before turning and she even looked at me again as she walked away.

An Unlikely Fooligan

Call me over sensitive or prone to getting things out of proportion or reading too much into things – whatever but her manner, I felt, said more than just being irritated by a lump of a foreigner. I felt that it wasn't me that this woman was really angry at but her past, her family, her country. It had been ruptured and broken and this was the feeling that she had to carry as she limped to her future days, the weight of defeat and disgrace bearing down upon her for infinity.

I looked down at the little plastic sheaf or wallet or whatever it's called and wondered where they were made, who made them and who bought them. I don't know why – it was a strange thing to think whilst on one's holiday. An idle thing to ponder and maybe the musing of a mind that is bored but that wasn't the case. No, it wasn't the case at all because a stirring formed in my stomach, a warmth that signalled an interest. It was an interest in the place that I was visiting. Like an anthropologist who had made a discovery, I was gaining an insight into the feelings of the indigenous people, of how some of them really felt and not the manufactured psyche that is commonly presented and I liked it. It suited my enquiring mind. I liked it a lot.

During those first few days of my second trip I had trouble getting my money changed into cash. It's probable that the situation has now altered but in 2003 that was the state of play around the Isehara area. The times when I could see a person who had the accredited qualifications to deal with my request to deal with my money became frustrating. Although I can't now remember everything it entailed, I do recollect the fuss and bother and the, what seemed to me, old fashioned system of communication and transfer and of having to wait lengthy periods of time and then the checking and double checking of my passport and other details. It was a trial.

I stayed in Isehara, taking the train to local places like Atsugi, Matsuda and Odawara. When there, I would amble about, sit in the bus station, watch the buses turning, look at the people, get struck temporarily deaf by the synthesis of high pitched hysterical voices coming from a passing swarm of schoolgirls, seemingly excited about nothing and I would seek out the cake shops. Searching out a good cake shop became a principal quest and the overweight man, the outsider, would sit content with a bag of the finest pastry sweet treats, going with the flow in perfect Taoist mode, being a natural to this Eastern experience, just looking different from those around me. But, that is accommodated by the way of things and the friendly people nodded and readily smiled as I made self-deprecating gestures to my eating cakes. Being the size of three of the people around me and tapping my belly would result in a hand shooting up to the mouth of the person who had smiled at me, cupping and concealing a laugh for it is rude but they shared and enjoyed my fun, the nomadic clown with the one 'fat man' joke but I didn't mind. No, I liked it. I liked it a lot.

I have a way about me where I'm often putting myself down. I do it to get by and I guess I'm too open when one considers we live in a world where the forked tongue speech seems to be the common currency. Being a stocky build, showing tattoos on my arms and having a straightforward manner often gives an impression to many that I am something that I am not. It's easier to read the labels that have been attached to someone I suppose.

I thought back to my first trip when having a walk in the evening with my friend's wife in Atsugi. Just as were going to cross a street, a car came to a sudden stop in front of us and the driver's door swung open. A man looked at us with a genial expression, he smiled and said something as he pointed at my arms. My friend's wife told me that he had noticed my tattoos. The man had a good look at me. He held up his hand showing that a piece was missing from his little finger. He smiled some more before bidding us farewell and went on his way. My friend's wife told me that she was frightened because the man was a member of a gang who made up the ranks of the Yakuza, the notorious Japanese gangsters. Of course I had heard of the Yakuza. They are known as the Japanese mafia and indeed this man was covered in tattoos, a trademark of their culture as is the practice of the ritual to cut off the end of the little finger.

"That's odd," I said to my friend's wife, meaning how the car stopped so suddenly and the man getting out. She told me that I stood out because of my bulky build and shaven head and, without being rude, told me that I can seem to people to be heavy. She told me that the Western males one usually encountered in Japan were usually academic and business suited types and didn't have this look and what with the coming of the World Cup, there had been a lot of media coverage regarding the English football hooligan. That was always pronounced as 'fooligan'. It was more than likely that this man thought I was one them making an early reconnaissance before the expected invasion of the shaven headed and tattooed brawling fooligans advanced onto Japanese soil. This wasn't to be the last encounter I was to have with gentlemen from the Yakuza ranks.

As I said, the World Cup took place on the year of my first trip and I'm sure if it hadn't my experience in TLOTRS would have been different because the response from people towards me wouldn't have been the same. My stocky frame and presence does cause some people to assume that I'm a bouncer type although the fooligan tag wasn't hanging around my neck during the time I spent in Japan on my second trip. Before I arrived on my first trip, my friend who I was to stay with in Isehara told me that the media in Japan was buzzing with expectation about English football supporters arriving on its shores. My friend had at that time lived in Japan seventeen years and had been and still is married to a Japanese woman. He works as a Professor in one of the universities. He is well travelled and has a good insight into the Japanese way of things. He told me that the Japanese attitude towards outsiders is very much that they are not Japanese and therefore to remain distinct from them. It is seen as an important part of Japan's resilience in retaining its proud autonomous status. They don't want their culture and race sullied with foreign and with what is often seen as inferior, blood. An island race. We've heard it before and there are methods of discouraging people to mix with outsiders but now Japan was centre stage as it hosted the World Cup and would be visited by different people from all over the world. And there was the English. They too would be coming and with it was the stigma that hangs over the English football fans of being violent troublemakers and all that goes with that. Apparently, a Japanese politician stood up in their version of the House of Commons and asked what was to be done with all the babies that were going to born in nine months time - a souvenir left to them by the visiting football fans!

The Japanese are seen as being polite and having courteous manners that, unfortunately, aren't common in other places and that led some to surmise that they would be run ragged by a marauding mass of English football thugs. The Japanese image of being vibrant and strong in the world of business had slipped as their economy had taken a bashing compared to ten years earlier but they were eager and proud to demonstrate that Japan would be the perfect host, having the stadiums, infrastructure, organisational skills and people who were interested and would give their full support in making it a good World Cup. Yet the question of the English remained a singular nut to crack. It became an international affair with British intelligence working with agencies in other countries, like Thailand for example, to prevent known troublemakers making lateral routes into the TLOTRS. My friend told me when talking on the telephone before I came over, that it is quite hilarious in the way that the English fans are being spoken about and perceived. He told me that there was constant coverage in the news of talking about what might happen, of how the country has prepared itself and the television showed mock up situations of rioting English fans as the country prepared to be ready if trouble actually happens. The scale of expectancy seemed out of all proportion as legions of militia practised tactics and hoards of people were dressed in English football shirts in the role play of football hooliganism. He told me the word 'fooligan' is used because 'hooligan' is difficult for Japanese people to pronounce and that in every news programme there was an item where the fooligan issue was discussed. He told me, 'Wait till you come over. You'll find it extremely amusing but mind, there will be those that might think that you are one of the fooligans. And he was right.

When I arrived, I sat in my friend's flat and saw on the television the preparations and grand display of vigilance because the fooligan would be making his entrance in a couple of weeks. There watching with me was my friend's wife, a diminutive Japanese lady wearing an England football shirt. The country had fully embraced the whole thing and had gone football crazy. The wearing of a different football nation's shirt was a common practice as well as wearing the Japanese one, of course. Many people wore an England shirt and what happened when England was knocked out of the competition? No worries. The shirt of a different nation would be worn although, through it all, David Beckham was placed on a pedestal and revered in his own right.

I sat there watching the stage managed riot control methods being practised to a backdrop of a running commentary having frenetic speech saying God knows what about the English but the word fooligan punctuated the speedy verbal discharge. As I watched it all, I became aware of something. Maybe I was wrong but I felt that the occasion had given the Japanese an opportunity to demonstrate a show of superiority over the slapdash, unruly mob of English/Westerners. The military-like planning was meticulous in its choreography and planning, running like a highly functional machine, each part gliding into place and performing at maximum capacity. It was an unstoppable force and one that could easily subdue any insubordination and as for foreigners who lack any substance, well, they were inconsequential weaklings that are brushed aside by a greater power that surpassed anything the facile outsider might present to them, the Japanese.

On the one hand it was amusing seeing the rehearsal for the invasion but other thoughts came to me whilst watching the spectacle of the sci-fi looking troop warriors brought to action in order to defend the country. The troop warriors descended professionally from flying crafts to scatter the weakling English troublemakers who do not know how to show respect and here, the fooligan is presented as the enemy, the outsider that will be vanquished and the fooligan is the essence of the foreign threat of intrusion. The Japanese haven't shown any preparations of might to be used against foreigners for a long time but now they are sanctified in doing so. I watched the acting abilities of those young Japanese men dressed in English football shirts playing the part of fooligans. I wondered where the authorities got them from. There were probably adverts put in papers and maybe many of them were drama students but their acting skills were not very good as their portrayal of football thugs was not accurate. They looked like hysterical laughing youngsters from a Japanese game show. Many of them were shaking their fists and shouting at the police/militia in the most unconvincing and absurd fashion and they couldn't stop laughing. They screwed up their faces in what was supposed to be aggression and then all turning as one, they ran from the State Riot Consultants who attacked them as they leapt from jeeps, armoured cars and helicopters.

I felt that the costume department and props had left reality as the troop warriors seemed to be dressed in outfits ranging from updated Roman Centurions to futuristic battle warriors. Some looked like they were from another world having black shiny costumes encasing their bodies that gave them a beetle like appearance, holding a shield in one hand and a baton in the other, their faces hidden behind visors. Some carried an assortment of guns, sprays, nets as well as other appliances of physical control. The Super Troopers ran into the skinny football shirted youngsters who giggled and slapped at one another in schoolchild excitement and again they turned and fled from the adults dressed as dark creatures representing the State Obedience Academy. There was also footage showing ranks of the sci-fi looking troop warriors in their uniforms all looking severe and grim faced, marching in lines eight in breadth, holding their batons in a salute style with their heads turned to one side and tilted upward. I reflected that I had seen that image before somewhere. It was a show of strength and of being in a state of readiness but I felt it also displayed something deeper. It gave the Japanese a stage to demonstrate their military preparedness and of how they are efficient in dealing with dissent and powerful in conflict. It showed Japan as victorious and in control. Although not a re-enactment of a Second World War battle scene, it did show the English as the enemy. How do these foreign intruders act?

An Unlikely Fooligan

Well, they drink until they can't stand, they shout abusive comments at anyone in range, they physically attack in cowardly acts, always a mob picking on one innocent passer-by, they vandalise and threaten. And all of this was acted out by the Japanese role players who had been employed to depict this anti-social behaviour in their own very inimitable style that is often seen in Japanese entertainment shows on television, each one of them slapping out their four limbs at once in an animated spectacle of imbecility and running as a mindless pack like headless chickens.

I wondered what the Japanese public thought as they watched this scene. There had to be those who enjoyed the drama as the Japanese fighting machine made their attack into the crowd, descending from flying crafts in their black centurion uniforms. Didn't they resemble, just for a second, the glorious and lamented Samurai Warrior? These brave faceless servants of law and order poured out from the ominous flying crafts that looked like dark creatures from another world that hovered close to the ground. There, in the cockpit, looking through his impenetrable visor is the all knowing General or Captain of order, monitoring the action going on beneath him, unmoving as he examines his brave State troops dispersing the childish English as they squealed and giggled and slapped out with their weak ineffectual limbs. The 'baton brothers' continued to move in, tossing stun grenades before them. They marched ever forward, entering the smoke but safe as they wore their masks and no part of their body was visible because the costume department had done their job well in designing outfits that gave the impression of representing an irrepressible force. No human effort would stand a chance in opposing the power of this State machine.

And so, it happened, the World Cup came and went and there was no battle scene and there were no rioting thugs. In fact, everyone enjoyed themselves and it was seen as maybe one of the great World Cups for atmosphere. Everybody celebrated the good times that can happen when people come together. I watched it on the television back home and read articles of how the Japanese police were giving stranded English supporters a lift back to their hotels. Bar owners apologised to the English revellers because they had ran out of beer, Japanese people were donning an England shirt and joining in the merriment because they enjoy and appreciate people having a good time. There were amusing stories like one I read of a Police Captain asking a man from the North of England who had collapsed outside a bar after about sixteen hours of solid drinking, if he felt unwell and could he be of any help in anyway.

Although it has to be said from what I saw, a lot of the louts were not out there. Thankfully the event was spared the presence of the contemptible type in their designer thug wear with their spiteful faces shielded by the peak of a baseball hat. Many of the England supporters looked a cross between cricket fans and people who play squash during their lunch break from the office. There weren't many exposed tattooed beer guts. No. That has to be said. This was the 'new man, footie' bunch who ape parts of a culture they had previously ridiculed. They'll indulge in having a beer and a pie but will offset the cholesterol and sodium content by altering something else in their diet. But and but with all that being said, it is often the people who aren't the trouble makers that are picked on and physically beaten by the police in other countries whilst following the England football team. All of them are seen as one and maybe, just maybe mind, it has something to do with those in other countries wanting to have a dig at the English for no other reason other than that they're English. And it has been disgusting how in the past, this kind of thing has been reported in our press. Now with the new footie fans, there are those in their ranks having influence from within the power structure of our media.

There was plenty of boozing and people reeling around the streets doing dance routines that were last done seriously in the holiday camp culture about fifty years ago. And I knew there wouldn't be any trouble and so did Chris who I stayed with in Isehara. We spoke about it before the World Cup started, agreeing in the main that the stigma attached to many football fans in the past came from those in the media that despised people because of who they were even though their actions haven't actually been harmful. Actions like lumping blokes who drink too much, acting the fool and boring people to death with their inane conversations but the point is, what they are doing is harmless. Those in the media often wrote for and represented a social type that had hardly any or no, positive referencing points with the experiences had by many football fans. A type was too simplistically constructed that was easy to demean, a type laden with negative aspects such as surly aggressive behaviour, racist, bullying, homophobic, sexist, vulgar, xenophobic, drunken and violent. Of course there was a lot of trouble surrounding football and there were and are more than enough bullying, imbecilic nasty cowards. It isn't by a big sweep, the full picture. Maybe the generalised English football thug was constructed to distinguish and amplify cultural differences and aspirations. He was a hyped up beast, residing in the minds of those working in the media and I believe has often been perpetuated by unimaginative, inexperienced and spiteful people who are blinded by their own ignorance and arrogance. They are wrong - so there.

The fooligan never came into being during the World Cup in Japan. The conflict didn't happen for several reasons. One of them, I believe, is that the Japanese authorities are more honest than where I come from. They come down heavily on people who are anti-social especially when physically harming an innocent passer-by or a vulnerable person. It is seen as important to be so. Therefore they won't allow entry into the country to those who are likely to be violent towards others. It can be seen as basic as that. They were not going to allow people into their country, take their money and moan about it afterwards when there has been trouble such as violence and vandalism. It's as if the western way wears the badge of freedom and liberty but its interests aren't with the average person. The State drops responsibility, letting the same people pay for the damage who had to suffer it to begin with; meaning the average person, whilst big businesses have made their profits without contributing to the clean up after the trouble has happened.

Another reason why there wasn't the expected trouble as my friend and I rightly predicted

is that, in general, we felt the Japanese would like the honesty of the average English football fan. I can tell you from experience from following the Fulham football team as a young boy that many football fans share a great deal of similarities with those following other great English hobbies such as train spotting which as one knows is a pastime that is often seen as inane with its participants as boring, maybe odd or quirky along with other discrediting terms such as a modern one used in common vernacular, 'anoraks'.

These people are often ridiculed because of their harmless pursuit. They have an interest that incorporates order, statistics, data, collection (that includes for both the football fan and train spotter: tickets, programmes, posters, autographs, photographs, books, videos, DVD's, particular clothing that are replicas denoting one's team or an item of clothing worn by railway staff, badges of teams or the various railways and lines, memorabilia related to both football and railways and so it goes on) travel, having membership to different societies and attending meetings where talks are given by eminent figures to a discerning assembly of railway enthusiasts or football fans. It is a personal pursuit but one that is shared with others. It brings one into contact with other fans or hobbyists and a structure exists where a pecking order takes place within that particular world.

The following of football is so diversified that there are people who follow a particular team week in week out and who just about have only one thing in common with others who do the same and that is that they watch a game of football because the experience, psyche and relationship to the community isn't a general one. For example, the cultural milieu inhabited by the non-league football follower bares little relationship with many of the people who follow a Premiership team. One's self identity is often associated with what team one supports. The absurdly priced tickets to see clubs in the Premiership are often, by silly buggers, a symbol of one's allegiance to the club and that they have the money because they earn well and they aren't losers like the dowdy and boring anorak types who go and watch lesser teams like those in the non-league. The supporters of the small clubs can derive a masochistic sense of pride because of their suffering, standing there in the mud, being frozen by a bitter wind and soaked through by persistent rain, talking about what team has the best programme, at what ground they had the best cup of tea, talking endlessly about such seemingly mundane things as, 'she only dipped the tea bag into the cup, barely coloured the milk and water' and then to discuss the date on the turnstile, a point of interest to a non-leaguer, denoting when it was made during the latter part of the industrial revolution. These are the things that are spoken about during the match and all the way home. Tenuous references are offered with a shaky knowledge of social history as that part of the country they are travelling to is talked about and when the team that they have come to see play goes yet another goal down, it's met by the travelling fan with a shrug of the shoulders and a moan that this is definitely the last time that they will pay good money and waste their time, coming to see the team that they have followed for years. But they will continue to follow and support them because like their distant brother or sister who takes his or her seat at the mega complex super stadium, they feel that they are part of the club and all it stands for.

The supporter, or follower, of the top teams enjoy the fact that the stand in which they have bought a ticket to sit holds as many people as the whole population of some towns that non-league football teams represent. The followers of a Premier league team will gladly buy the merchandise in the club superstore and the identity of the team is extended as they buy Birthday and Christmas presents for family and friends and household items that have the club's name and colours on them and the names and faces of those players that are significant in marketing the club's image will adorn their homes, cars and beings.

At the moment there is the fad for talking about footballers' wives, their shopping habits, backgrounds in modelling and maybe the charity work that they do. They may also endorse products, their stories are sold to newspapers and magazines, the inside of their homes and sometimes the estates where they live are opened up to different media channels for those members of the public who are interested to see where and how they live. The high flying footballer is part of the modern celebrity phenomena where fashion and money is the entrance fee to a way of life that has echelons of statuses in itself and an industry called the paparazzi is now a term that is commonly seen and heard in the media. The footballer has an agent as does his wife and their children are often involved in this circus at a very young age as daddy is in the papers for being involved in a scuffle outside a nightclub and features in a 'kiss and tell' story in a newspaper that has been written for an aspiring model whose agent has already secured her place on a new game show on the strength of the allegation. The high powered cars, recreational drugs and all the contemporary hedonistic rewards that are thrown at the footballer in the top league fades to the insipid reality that is experienced by those playing at the other end of the spectrum. The children of those who support top clubs often judge their peers by what teams they are aligned with. And so from an early age, the process of socialisation evolves as allegiances and stigmas are created and with it the personal identities that are being formed by those children.

In my experience of being dragged to see Fulham football club as a boy, I was aware of the aching boredom that took up most of the experience, from the journey to the game, the match itself and the return journey home. I'm talking primarily about away games. When returning to school on Monday morning, some of the youngsters would ask if I had been to a football game. At that time my team were playing in towns most of the youngsters had never heard of, so cries of derision and taunts of ridicule would be shouted. Although associating with the game of football, a lot of youngsters suffer the same belittling treatment that say a youngster who was interested in the history of steam trains, metal constructs and bus timetables. Over the years I have heard and read in the press descriptions of football fans as if nearly all of them were thugs out for a fight and who were racist, sexist, homophobic and have political leanings to extreme right wing fascist organisations. If these ignoramuses that reside in their bubble of condescension who disseminated this falsity had ever experienced or had the interest to find out what life is really like for the people that they wrote about, they would indeed discover that, in the main, things are very different. The work of the journalist can be used to demonise and construct the other for purposes I'm not going into here but the point is, why let the truth get in the way of lies and myths if they serve the purposes of intent?

It certainly wasn't my experience to be in the company of nasty bully boys when travelling to an away game with the faithful. I was with men and a few women who were pilgrims, full of blind faith, giving their time and money. They travelled on the coach or by train, the ladies knitting, the sandwiches packed, men in deep discussion but being guarded to hold back certain information that they felt might be advantageous to the person that they are talking to because it was often a competitive affair as statistics were compared and notebooks with carefully titled pages having principal points underlined in a different coloured pen or pencil were examined and shown and then scrutinised. I would gaze out of the window of the train, my sandwiches already eaten and we were only twenty minutes into the journey and listen to a discussion between two men. 'You had cheese sandwiches last time we played in Stockport' or 'No, no, no, it rained on the day of the Northampton game – in fact it was the wettest day for over a hundred years. I know that because I heard it on the radio that night; I was in bed listening to the World Service'.

Football programmes were kept in protective plastic covers and one or two were bought for people who didn't come to the game and maybe never came to a game of football but collected the programmes. Detailed knowledge of people involved with the club was known with things like specific details of the way the grounds man was doing his job and what train line on the tube he takes to get to the ground. The complaints that had been lodged regarding the price of the tea and snacks were debated and the quality of the pastry would be a talking point as rows of drenched terraced houses passed by outside the window of the train. The industrial past of the country was talked about as large chimneys were spotted in an environment that was very different from that where we came from in the London area. Then the London centric loftiness would raise itself as Northerners were spoken about as a backward species and their accent, the food that they ate and the way that they lived were discussed.

And I would look out of the window and try to imagine the people that lived there and had lived there to make the place what it was. I thought about their history and their experience and we, the travelling football supporters, were cocooned in a speeding metal construction, taking us to one of these outposts and I would become excited at the prospect of seeing and feeling a different experience. From what I had been listening to during the journey, I had conjured up images of difference. As we pulled into the station that was our destination, further comments were made regarding the remains of the industrial town that we had arrived at. But it was us that were the clueless ones and through ignorance we shaped people from typecasts that had been presented by others. On alighting from the train, I discovered that in fact the place resembled many aspects of what I was familiar with. The accent was different and the names of certain things had a regional name and maybe a newspaper would be a different colour but the air felt the same, maybe a bit chilly to what I was used to and the women, as at home, struggled with shopping bags in the town centre and I would then try and see a difference, looking into the faces of people. Even studying the way a cat or dog walked. What was said on the journey about the people and the places that we were travelling to was mostly rubbish.

The return journey would begin with an atmosphere that was a little animated as if we were an army that were triumphant in having performed a mission in enemy territory. Stories were told of what was said to the man working on the turnstile or selling the programmes or selling the tea and snacks. It was usually lies but harmless as the teller of the unlikely tale recounted the imagined experience of tearing a strip off the people in their scenario, lecturing them on manners and decency, telling them their place and sometimes even physically threatening them. Of course the backward provincial person would back down.

I remember on one occasion, as the train was pulling from the station to take us home, a man took from his pocket a piece of food that he had bought in the town we had just been to. It was done in a way as if it had been successfully smuggled across a dangerous border crossing and it was placed upon the table for examination. I think it was a pie or it could have been a sausage roll. Anyway, parts of the piece of food was pointed at and grave tones of speech were used as descriptions were made about the unpleasantness of the whole thing. There was an inquiry and slow nods of agreement moved heads that supported a notion that something must surely be done about this serious matter. It was then gathered up and thrown in the rubbish bag that a woman had with her. Where it belongs and that was that. Hands were brushed. Any remnants of the offending piece were now put in the past as was the town that we had travelled to that day. The match was almost also forgotten because it would have been a drab affair that usually ended in a loss or draw.

I remember those people, the unlikely hooligans making the pilgrimage, heads down in concentration as public transport timetables were checked to see if connections could be made and conversations took place of what they were going to have for tea when they got in that night. There was always one of them who would quickly take a notebook from his pocket and write down the number of a shunting engine as it passed through a station that we had stopped at and he would go on to tell the people around him what stock it was and where it was built. And as I sat there in the train, I imagined how the team that we had travelled to see were making their way home. It would be in one of those luxury coaches that I had seen parked outside the grounds, the seats facing each other with a little table between them. I was told that the players played cards on the table. I tried to create an image of the players. Because I was a boy, they looked like men but most of them were really just older boys in their smart suits and fashionable hairstyles, giving a brief wave and a nod out of the window to some fans that chanted their name. Then they would look around to the other players that they were sitting with and carry on their conversation. I wondered what it was that they were saying.

These are memories that I have. These are little fragments of my experience and feelings that make up the whole.

Four

So, as I sat in the bus station at Odawara, I remembered back to those days going to see Fulham. Things were different this year because the World Cup experience of the year before had desensitised the Japanese to the physical spectacle of stout Englishmen with shaven heads having tattoos. A year before, looks would linger but now I wasn't such a strange exhibit so Mr Pastry ambled on buses and trains, showing his map and consulting the trusted phrase book that he had bought the year before and not to be asked again, hopefully, if he was fooligan. I grinned to myself as I thought about this, of the occasions during my trip the previous year when young people looked and some pointed and older people gave me long probing stares.

After a few days I rang my friend Jon, the chap who was working and lived in central Tokyo. After the usual difficulties of establishing what station to get out of and where to meet, we did successfully find each other on a street corner next to a well known multinational coffee house near to where he worked which was one of those concrete and glass mountains inhabited by one of the main banks in the financial district of Tokyo. He took me to some obscenely expensive bars and restaurants, the type of places that most of us have heard people talk about when discussing Tokyo. Not that I paid. These City chaps earn well and have the card to flash where the company provides the cash. We then went to a bar where there were no Japanese people and then to another one. These places are expatriate haunts. Nearly all the people in them had moved to Tokyo with their jobs but there are a few who have stayed and revolve in a twilight world making a living in drinking holes serving the financier nomads as they socialise in their quality time. The people having this way of life are made up of an assorted mix having a common culture of being on the make. It wasn't something I travelled to be part of, to stand in a bar six thousand miles away with the guys in a designer footie set, complete with wearing the team's colours. Some of the things I observed within this lifestyle were absurdly funny. Well, I thought they were.

During my first trip my friend and his wife had decided to stay in central Tokyo for one night over the weekend. He thought it would give me an insight into what's going on in the world of expatriate activities and although knowing I'm a miserable sod, it would at least give me the experience. We arrived in central Tokyo in the early evening and went to a well known haunt for the expatriate financier types, the name of it I'm not even going to try and remember. It was some inane theme type of chain bar thing. Remember, this was just before the World Cup and Japan was bracing itself for the invasion of English football thugs.

"Here they come," I heard someone say. The remark was aimed at me and connected with the expected influx of English football fans. I looked over and saw this reptilian looking English bloke with the Bermondsey 'barra' accent looking at me, his saurian like eyes settling on me. I cast him a glare. I didn't like the look of this chap and his slippery stare fell away from me. There was a television crew roving around town wanting to interview the English football followers, hoping to get a story and images of the pink skinned monsters revelling in beer, blood and bellicosity. A couple of expatriate types asked me if I was over for the football, telling me that the television and in fact all the media, was revved up in anticipation and selling stories that warned of trouble. I was told of past football tournaments and of how the foreign news people pay English fans to act in loutish ways just so they can get a story so it would be best to ignore anyone approaching me with a camera and microphone. I looked around the place that I was standing in, having to remind myself that I was actually in Japan. Although the people in the bar weren't unfriendly, it wasn't what I wanted. I was on holiday only for a short time and I really didn't want to spend it there. The Australian barmaid exchanged clichéd lines that passed as humour and nearly everything that was said came from television programmes and in vogue films with South African young men dressed in their 'time out' clothing who exchanged tips to English people about awesome places in the world where adults can play in the snow on boards. The bungee jumping New Zealander checked the strength of the grip of a bloke from Scotland and there were more cockney accents shouted over each other than a bar scene in an episode of Eastenders, that well known British television soap for dopes.

"Way to go," someone shouted and a carefully styled ladette, complete and faithful to the designers that engineered her presentation, let out a string of expletives while keeping a self-conscious eye on all in her range because her raucous posturing couldn't hide her insecurity. From there we went to the inevitable Irish pub and I'll leave it to you to conjure up what that was like. We then made our way to a bar that was well known and might still be. It was on some floor in a building that is reached by a lift that was so small I found it hard to imagine that drinkers out on a spree wouldn't lose patience having to wait for the lift and then not being able to get inside it. My friend and his wife told me that the bar was one of 'the' places to go for the expatriates. We stepped into the lift and my friend knew that I wasn't impressed or that interested. When the doors of the lift opened I was startled to see a group of people standing behind a bar staring at us whilst cheering and waving their arms in the air. They acted in that fake hysterical way that I saw as a child on American game shows. In fact they were the only places that I saw people act like that.

And then the false corporate hospitality quickly diminished and the pretence of joy faded from their faces. I hadn't seen a more facile expression of insincerity and hollow worth but this is the generation and type socialised to team building, group dynamics and designer interaction. It wasn't a large place and there were only two or three other people in there. It wasn't late and the good drinking cash hunters hadn't yet broke out of the lift to party. Later in the evening the place is turned into a desperate kind of scene where the highly charged emotions clutch at excesses to satisfy one's inner emptiness. The bar staff came from different continents and it goes without saying there were none from Japan. They were all dressed in footie shirts denoting different countries. The World Cup was imminent and these guys were ready for it because everything's fun but their dour faces reflected other concerns as they paced behind the bar, checking the time until lift off. My attitude and looks showed my disinterest and although polite to the barman when he asked me if I was over for the footie, we didn't engage in conversation.

I was told stories of drinking games played by the expatriates and of how the bar staff are an integral part of the proceedings, chanting 'higher, higher' urging more to be spent, watching the bar bill rising as it is displayed on a large screen so that others can see the money being sucked from the credit card that is inserted into a machine. The bar staff would raise their arms and cheer as the patron buys more drink and reputations are made by the customer who isn't an 'ex'- prat at all as his or her behaviour clearly shows. But enough already; God, I'm a miserable sod.

I left my friend and his wife that night and went out walking around the streets making up the area where the night-time entertainment is to be found. Although Japan is essentially racially homogeneous, in this area there are people from other countries milling about trying to make a living from the entertainment industry. I thought it out of place when a Nigerian young man was quite pushy in trying to impose upon me something or other. It wasn't drugs but something to do with going into a club. I asked him where it was that he came from and how long he had been in Japan. He gave up trying to pitch whatever his business was and gave me a good look over. He told me that I was 'the man' and asked me what I was doing. I was bored with all that crap and so I ambled off, having a small beer in a couple of places, very mindful to check the price first. The back street bars were best, of course.

Anyway, getting back to my second trip and going up to see my friend who works for a bank. We had a good night. I'm lucky. As with my other friend, Jon was a very good host and being a generous person he wanted me to have a look at things that he knew I wouldn't see if I wasn't with him. I stayed round his place that night and I must say it was a very impressive flat on the twenty fourth floor looking over central Tokyo. After idling around the next day, I took the train out to Isehara. I had decided to stay there for the weekend before setting off on a train journey. I found my way back amongst the throng of commuters. The jet lag hadn't left me which muddles the concentration when trying to find the correct line or track. My friend and his wife were away for the weekend and I was to have a drink in a bar that was local to where they lived. It was a bar that I liked.

Five

There is a small bar in Isehara which to me, really fits the image and feel of a setting in a foreign land. It emulates an American bar having a jazz feel, set somewhere around the 1950's in some side of Chicago or New York. It is a small bar. Whiskey is the favoured drink, served on ice in a long glass, drunk just like Sinatra might have done in a film where he was called 'Johnny' or 'Joe' and smoke lay in the air like a heavy mattress in a whore's bedroom. The guys sat up against the bar, mostly entering and leaving by themselves. Discussion usually consists of cynical grunting and then the head that was raised to engage the brief interaction is again lowered and the eyes re-set themselves. Vision is adjusted to that place somewhere in some distance that lone men look into when drinking. The bar was a local for my friend who lived in Isehara and although in recent years not being such a frequent visitor, it had been a haunt of his. From what I knew, he was the only foreigner in there but he was well accepted by the man who owned this curious and modest little establishment. Because of its quirkiness and the incorrigible character of the man who owned the place, it became a favourite of mine. I don't know his real name but I called him Master Samurai.

Master Samurai is a man of stubborn nature and having a personality that upsets people especially as he hasn't moved with the times in his attitude towards women even in a culture that hasn't really adopted the post feminist agenda in a way that would be comparable to say the United Kingdom, for example. The bar is situated on the first or second floor of a drab looking grey concrete building above shops in a side street not far from the station area. Once reaching the cramped and dingy landing, a small door when pushed open, leads to a darkened bar having an amber glow that is characteristic of a late night jazz scene. I would say that the place, on average, had six or seven people in there, most of them locals. It is hardly ever a port of call for a woman to stop at. I suppose it was easy to see why women didn't go in there what with Master Samurai's manner, his customers' rigidity in changing their habits, their suppressed hostility and an indifference towards women if they did actually enter and sully the place with their banal and loquacious chattering, light laughter and garish dress!

It seemed fitting that Master Samurai was a big fan of Samurai warriors. I don't think it was in an academic historian kind of way but in having interests in reading magazines and watching films that deal with the subject. The word Samurai means 'to serve' which is apt for a person who owns a bar and serves customers drinks. Yet, Master Samurai isn't too honourable in his approach to hospitality and of welcoming customers to his little bar. During my first trip I asked my friend if the bar ever got full. He told me that it didn't and that Master Samurai actively discouraged any great numbers of people entering. I was told of a time when a coach party had turned up and although the place was nearly empty, Master Samurai became quite hostile and he turned the people away telling them that the bar was closing. It was a simple matter that he just didn't want that many people in the bar and to be harassed by them wanting drinks.

An Unlikely Fooligan

I watched Master Samurai as my friend told me this tale and other stories of his lack of congeniality towards people who wanted to have a drink in his own little establishment. It was his own private bar. It was his after all and so he should be allowed to say who he wants to enter. I liked him and as I observed him busying himself behind the counter mixing just the one drink for a known local. I began to like him a lot and then he looked up and caught me looking at him. He smiled and gave the customary nod and I reciprocated for I also find it natural to smile and nod. My friend told me that Mr Samurai liked me. He had told my friend so. It was rare for him to like people but it was so. He thought I looked like a film star, maybe Bruce Willis. It was bizarre and I liked it all the more. Master Samurai had and maybe still has, a wife. I didn't see her but I was told that she used to work at the bar. My friend told me that she was different from her husband in that she was quite friendly to people and enjoyed a chat but because of the frustration that she felt by his reluctance to create a place of more conviviality and suffering the tedium of many of the customers ways and also the absence of female company; well, it caused her to stay at home which I was told pleased Master Samurai.

I visited the bar with my friend and his wife during my first trip and although my friend had tired of going there, I told him that I liked it. It fitted my quirky sense of things and I liked the individualistic character that was Master Samurai as I got to call him. The drinks were expensive but when paying for my tab, I found that it hadn't cost me much at all. My friend told me it was because Master Samurai had bought me a few himself. I looked up and sure enough, there he was, looking at me and nodding. A smile was covering most of his face yet I felt that behind his eyes were questions that he wanted answers to because at heart he wasn't the cynical diehard misery who had closed up his emotional shop and stop wanting to make any new discoveries or having a sense of adventure. I saw or believed that I saw that Master Samurai was in fact just bored. He was bored with his life, routine and surroundings and that he wanted to know about life in that other world; that world where those 1950's and 1960's American jazz musicians came from and those films where 'Johnny' or 'Joey' 'No Good' came from, the land of diners, drive in cinemas, burgers and shakes, trilby hats, lonesome cowboys, cattle drives that went on for weeks in a landscape that seemingly went on for ever, the Saint Valentine's massacre, Jack Dempsey and big men gorging themselves on beef steaks the size of a karaoke stage, where there is grid iron and guys that can pitch a fast ball as speedy as any bullet train – from the Californian playground with a golden sun and young tanned bodies lazing and playing to a sound of beautiful music having background harmonies smoother than the finest kimono silk, a place where women are wild and will seduce you in a bar where a blind piano player whose ancestors were shipped to the Land of the Free as slaves tinkers tunes that tell of heartbreak and lost love and these women have legs that climb higher than any building restriction will allow in Tokyo because of earthquakes and a person can find a buddy on one of the highways that travel from forests of neon where there is the promise of excitement that lives in the metropolitan dream to a terrain of isolation and where everyone is a stranger. It is a wilderness of wonders but it is an image emanating from just after the Second World War.

And here, in his little bar, Master Samurai is proud of Japanese tradition and culture, principally the Samurai who were not just defenders of authority but were men having their own esteemed culture, understanding aesthetics as much as being accomplished in combat but through it all, Master Samurai has a deep seated wanting for 'American Joe' and some of his ways, a yearning to ease back in Sloppy Joe's and relax in that seemingly carefree flow of things that are American. He saw it as the land of excess and the men seemed insouciant, not having the binds to responsibilities and the concerns that he had experienced in the cramped, meagre and guilt ridden culture that was his own. Those dark eyes, although outwardly impenetrable, couldn't hide or conceal the boyish hunger that he held for the American. His face looked more like a child's than a middle-aged man's as his smile washed away the stuffy years and his mind exploded in the glittering world of famous actors and actresses with the lavish productions and pomp that exists in a world that the film factory saw as their own to exploit and indulge in. There are the big bands, the crooners, musicians and Marylyn Monroe whose wide hips and accommodating lips symbolised the lavish. He knows that the younger people in his own country follow the modern import from America but for him it's just a noise without real talent, not having the substance held by the icons of his early childhood that was set in an imagery propagated by the new imperial masters. He came out of his trance, the place where he retreated to ponder and fantasise over Americana and he regained his poise and sense of place and being. He was in his bar, again. Yes, the bulky Westerner had hit a chord that resounded the tunes that played constantly beneath the surface. I nodded again and Mr Samurai nodded back and smiled, giving me a thumbs up gesture for communication was extremely limited. His smile broadened and the dream had gone from his features. Normal living had resumed but he continued to look at me. It was as if he didn't want to let this chance go of finding out more about the Western way and who knows, his life just might change. Although always thought of as an impossible dream, just maybe he would go to that land. He wanted to speak to someone that he felt held the key to explaining and showing him the way but he didn't know how to ask those questions and now I had come along and maybe he had a link to that world he so sought information about.

During one of our first chats, I discovered that Master Samurai was dissatisfied with TLOTRS. I had told him through the interpreting skills of my friend, that I liked Japan and that there are many things better in Japanese culture than in the place where I come from but he told me that he wanted to go to the West. "You smile," he told me in bold physical gestures, telling me that I smile easily and that I am happy and that it is different for me because in Japan people are miserable. "You are like....., erm, film star!" I told Master Samurai that he couldn't be more wrong and that I am known for being a miserable sod and that people in London, New York, Chicago and Las Angeles have to endure the same pressures that he and his customers come up against and in some ways it's worse when one considers the fear of violence felt in the West. This stopped Master Samurai. He considered what I was telling him but he didn't seem convinced; after all there had been well over forty years of delusion at play in his poor old Tokyo mind. He winced and shook his head at what I was saying as if what I had said might be true but all the same, there was something missing in TLOTRS and it exists in TLOT-Free.

Whilst visiting bars in Japan, I was called 'Jumbo' a few times but it was in Master Samurai's bar that I was first referred to by this name by the man himself. When he first said the name it was like he was testing the water because the Japanese are known for socially polite manners. But I didn't mind. In fact I played on it because it provided a bridge for purposes of communication to take place when ordinarily it is very difficult to do so. I hammed it up, slapping my belly, puffing out my chest, making a playful grab for Master Samurai and he played his part by jumping out of the way in a fashion performed in the over acting style of an American wrestler. He stood with his hands on his hips and widened his eyes at such a spectacle and I growled, making myself bigger and shouting "Sumo". Master Samurai clapped his hands and fell about laughing at such intellectual wit and imagination; but it was only fun and I learned that the Japanese like slapstick humour and also like people who have the ability to poke fun at themselves. It held me in good stead whilst I travelled around the country and meeting people during the two visits that I made.

Master Samurai asked me if I knew anything about the Samurai. I told him that I didn't but when I was eighteen years old I went to the cinema in Leicester Square in London's busy West End with an Italian man who was dating my sister to see a film called The Seven Samurai. The Italian was a film buff and told me that it was a classic. Well, Master Samurai was very impressed. He went to a room at the back of the bar and returned with posters of the very film. He watched me carefully as I examined the posters, looking for any emotion and, as mad it might seem, I felt that Master Samurai was thinking that he had at last met an outsider, a person coming from that world who he could connect with. A bright smile was embedded into his face, unflinching as his dark eyes sparkled with joy.

On those visits to his bar during my first trip, Master Samurai relaxed with me. He had found a buddy and we goofed around, having a slapstick routine that we shared, just like maybe Chuck and Glen or Joey and Johnny, those American characters that he had seen in films and had read about in magazines. He invited me behind the bar to serve some drinks to customers, showing me where the single malt scotch was and how much mixer was used to make another drink, all the while watching me as a father proudly watches his son, grinning and cracking into instant laughter at some clumsy action I might have made. He turned to the customers but they didn't share such fun at seeing Jumbo lumber childishly behind the bar. They retained their sullen indifference but now questioning the sanity of the man that they had known for years as being more moody and cheerless than all of them. But here he was, like an excited adolescent, with his new friend. I got him in a headlock and he played to a gallery that wasn't there, only the line of lone men looking over their drinks as they always do, only this time watching the antics of a man they thought that they had known. I could sense the seemingly innate antipathy felt by the customers towards the foreigner and here, in all the places he should be showing himself with such crude abandon but this was lost on Master Samurai. On one occasion, he pointed at me and told me that he would go to America with me. "To Chicago," he said. I told him that I come from London in England and this momentarily confused him as he nodded and swallowed this information for later contemplation.

My knowing about or having heard of Samurai and having the willingness to talk about it further confirmed our good relationship. I told him that my brother's wife had asked me to look out for the little charms that the Samurai warrior wore on his belt. She knew that nowadays they would probably be marketed as touristy trinkets so it was fortuitous bumping into Master Samurai because I was sure that he would know what I was on about. He was very interested in my sister-in-law and wanted to know how she knew of such things and that indeed he had many of these charms. I told him that she wasn't an expert on the history of the Samurai but she has an eye for interesting and artistic things and that she liked what she had seen of Japanese paintings. Master Samurai seemed proud as he gave me some charms, telling me that they were replicas of what the Samurai warriors wore around their belts. They were small plastic mouldings of grotesque faces and bodies, rats being one of the images. I kept one for myself and still have it tied on the indicator switch in my car. It is of a monstrous looking baby holding a drumstick. They are supposed to evoke spirits that will protect and I believe Master Samurai believed this to be so. Who am I to say different?

Master Samurai closed his bar on Sundays but on the afternoon of that day he would sometimes hold a private gathering of selected people to join him and watch old Samurai films, mostly on 8mm film. Although there was alcohol behind the bar, he wouldn't serve any on that day and if anybody wanted to drink they had to bring their own as he did even though he was the owner of the bar and had bought the stock that was a few feet away from where he would be sitting watching the films. It wasn't anything to do with a licensing law and it being a Sunday - it was just his law. I was told by my friend that there are some who had been regular drinkers in the bar for years but had never been invited to one of the viewing sessions. Although my friend had been invited it wasn't really his thing but he thought that he had to go because it would offend Master Samurai if one declined the invitation. In fact everyone he knew who had attended the sessions felt it a duty to do so. So when I was invited for a Sunday afternoon session of watching the films, my friend told me that I was privileged but I had to make sure that I arrived on time and bring my own drink.

I was glad that Master Samurai had invited me. I looked forward to the unusual experience. After all, here I was in Japan being invited to partake in a ritual organised by this singular man. I like characters so I bought a few cans of beer and headed up to Master Samurai's bar on that Sunday. But when reaching the landing, I couldn't open the door that led to the bar. I knocked and called out but nobody came. I did wonder if I had come at the wrong time as I couldn't hear any sounds from inside. So, I returned to my friend's place telling him of my failed adventure. He told me that there was an outer door that they locked and that one had to press a buzzer but it was now too late to go there. I saw Master Samurai later in the week and told him this. He was very apologetic, taking me outside to the landing and with the use of sign language explaining what to do if I came again. He shook his head disappointedly and turned to a disinterested man who was a regular customer ruing the fact that Jumbo didn't attend the viewing session. I took it that was what he was saying because Jumbo was the only word I understood. The local man nodded. He wasn't interested and when Master Samurai had finished speaking and turned away, the customer looked at me. He didn't nod an acknowledgement but his look told me that I had a lucky escape.

I'm sure that I am correct in saying that I enjoyed Master Samurai's bar more than my friend did. It was new to me and after all my friend had lived there for years. One evening I went along to the bar by myself and started speaking or rather indulged in broken communication with a young woman. It was strange to see a woman in there. She told me that she was a local and was fully aware of Master Samurai's character and that she knew my friend whom I was staying with. The young woman was keen to try out her English. She had an education in business studies if I remember correctly and had that American slur to her accent. She asked how I liked Asia. This confused me for a second as I didn't think of Japan as being in Asia. I know that sounds absurd because I was obviously in Asia and it showed my ignorance and the way I stereotype. It was because of the affluence, the self-reliance and indulgence of material consumerism that exists in Japan. It didn't fit the ready image that I had of Asia where I imagined poverty to be the common experience. She, I keep saying 'she' because I have forgotten her name, was a bright young women and I'm sure that she looked at me as if I was a bit on the dim side but she was pleasant and interested in my story as I was in hers. I looked over at Master Samurai who was looking over at me. He was shining a glass and he nodded with no change of expression but if there was a gesture to be found it said, "everything's okay and she'll be leaving soon because she's not much of a drinker".

When making arrangements for my second trip, I picked up a couple of trinkets to give Master Samurai. One was of a London Bobby, the other of a Beefeater. They were the obvious kind of touristy thing and when I gave them to Master Samurai I could see that he was very pleased with the thought. He placed them carefully in a space behind the bar and I was sure that they would be there for a long time. The giving of little presents to people around oneself is a common thing to do in Japan. I wasn't aware of this custom when I bought the little gift as I have always liked doing it as well and this was further reciprocated when Master Samurai produced a red grapefruit from under the counter, telling me to have it and to take it home with me.

The morning of the day that I was going on my travels, I saw Master Samurai in one of the local stores. He was busy and I felt that he was looking impatient as he bought his groceries. When I tapped him on his shoulder, he turned and on seeing that it was me, he roared with laughter exclaiming "Jumbo". It appeared out of place for him seeing me in the shop and for me he also looked out of place, away from his domain where he was the principal character but here he was, an inconspicuous person who was just part of the common flurry. We shook hands. The communication was poor as I told him that I was heading off that day on my travels using the train pass. He wished me well and that was the last I saw of him during my trip. I didn't know at that time that I wouldn't be returning to Isehara.

Bumping into Master Samurai had given me an interest to read up about the Samurai and in doing so gave me more of an understanding to the Japanese psyche. The Samurai tradition involved the practice of servitude, loyalty, respect, etiquette, discipline, ritual and an appreciation of fine aesthetics in the arts and other areas of learning, as well as being skilled in physical combat. The Buddhist philosophy spread through Samurai culture, influencing beliefs and shaping values regarding death, fear and killing. As the use of the Samurai warrior as a protector diminished so did the powers, status and rights that they had. Those coming from Samurai backgrounds integrated into normal society. A popular field to have a presence in was bureaucracy. Their influence is felt in Japanese culture. Although symbolic rather than pragmatic, the Samurai are still an important part making up the whole.

And so that Monday morning I was going on a trip by train by myself. I thought of the 'wave man' - that is the translation of the word describing a Samurai warrior who becomes separate without being part of a clan and having no attachments. He was known as a Ronin, (wave man); he who has to wander alone aimlessly for ever – I hope not.

Six

With my stuff packed I said farewell to my friend and his wife in Isehara. At that time thinking that I would see them again but it was not to be; it was just a case of circumstances. My friend was a very informed host having a great knowledge of Japanese culture and an interest in getting about the country. He gave me directions of how to get to a hotel in Kyoto once out of the station. I could sense that he had some concern although not having major reservations or seriously worried about my welfare but it can get confusing travelling around a place where there is little or no understandable language to communicate with. There are now signs in English in the cities but then there were hardly anything. Once out of the main areas of Tokyo there was nothing and in the country parts, I would be an exhibit.

Although the Japanese have the reputation for politeness, I found that there are those that make no show of hiding their curiosity and suspicion by openly staring for a long period. Even in the land of concealment I was to be ogled at. I think one of the reasons why my friend had some concern was that I am not the ordinary traveller type who would book into a place used by other traveller types and go to bars and places frequented and known for the foreign person on holiday or the outsiders who live there. No. He knew I would drift to the margins of the standard text on the page, go to places and meet people not usually visited and whilst I would most probably be safe because I had been around different places and people and Japan was a safe place, I could sense that my friend was slightly uneasy about something. It showed by the shade of doubt on his face. Maybe he just felt responsible for me, I don't know but off I went and caught my first train which was a local train taking me to Odawara where I could catch the bullet train south.

As is the case with many people, I like travel or the thought of it. It gives a slight purring of excitement in one's stomach. When waiting for the bullet train after going through the muddle to find out what platform or track the train will be arriving at from Tokyo, I bought myself something to eat. It was a treat, I pondered to myself, for I had bought a bento box containing the complete lunch set of sushi, rice and other things from the little cabin on the station platform. The look and taste was different. It was a Japanese experience and here I was waiting to catch a bullet train and partaking in the fare commonly eaten by the indigenous people. It gave me the feeling that I was in a different land, walking amongst people with overtly different customs and away from the standardised culture presented through the mammoth companies that have eaten into nearly everywhere and everything. Even though all that is evident in Japan, there also exists a difference.

As I thought about this difference, my mind went back to the previous year when my friend had booked a weekend stay in an Onsen (natural hot springs). The place he had pre-booked is in a town called Matsuzaki, a hot spring resort and a very nice place it is as well. The baths are separated according to one's sex and in the particular place that we were staying, there was an outdoor bath, pool affair and what with looking at the local surroundings whilst immersed in the warm water, it is a very pleasurable experience. The establishment that we stayed in had a dress code. One is given – they are left in one's room – a ceremonial looking jacket that one wears to come down to breakfast. It is not dissimilar from a short dressing gown but looking more oriental and martial arty. There are also wooden flip-flops that one can wear and in fact a person can withdraw from the modern Western presentation of self and relax in an atmosphere of a time and culture that most would think as being lost and gone; yet I am glad to say that it hasn't. As everywhere that I went, the establishment was very clean and the food well presented by people who seemed professional in doing their work and who themselves were wholesome in personal cleanliness and appearance. Hygiene is a priority in Japan and later I will have a grumble about the hypocrisy in the West, especially the place where I come from, where matters such as food hygiene have become an industry in itself although food poisoning is on the increase.

Now the reader of this little rambling will have to excuse me for not using the correct terms and words when describing some of things that I came across. I know that maybe I should have done some research to find out what they are but I feel by not doing so keeps the mystique and maintains the feeling of difference one encounters when going to a place that one has liked. The hotel, if that's the name it's known as, that we stayed in reminded me of something out of the 1950's. The interior hadn't been assaulted in efforts to keep up with in-vogue furnishing and the like but rather retained a space of sedate repose and possibly offered a modest celebration of tradition and culture. Most of the people that were staying there were not the young who were in search of night-time amusements and beating the drum for modern and predictable pursuits but rather it was an older clientele who visited the resort to unwind and immerse themselves in the Japanese experience and good judges they are too.

We took the express train from Isehara and then a bus to the west coast of the Izu Peninsular. The distance from central Tokyo is about a hundred miles I suppose but it takes a while because of catching different trains and the bus weaves itself around small roads. The trip gave me an opportunity to look at a more traditional view of Japan. Miles of rice fields stretched both sides of the road and as we rolled through this landscape, my friend's wife explained to me the process of irrigation and of how the land is managed. The people looked different from those that I had seen in the tiny amount of time I had been in the country. I liked this side of things, it was Japanese and after all that's what I had come to experience. The country people had that rough look of those who earn their living by manual agricultural work. Their appearance, dress and lack of cosmetic aesthetics denotes another life, a hard life probably but I feel there is an honesty and I have found that they have more time to give to a person. The areas for cultivating rice are cut into the sides of hills, giving the landscape an appearance that one has seen on the side of some young peoples' heads as they leave the hairdressers. Etched into the mud is a carefully layered pattern weaving itself across the now styled terrain.

As the bus continued its climbing and downward spirals through the countryside, I looked at the appealing scenery. The little mountains on the peninsular reminded me of baby mountains. There were clouds misting the tops of them and whereas large mountains wrench themselves from the ground, these were a far more genteel affair. The humble little mountains were neat and unassuming having bright green vegetation covering them and little hamlets or maybe just a few houses that resided seemingly peacefully amongst the attractive range. The clouds looked like they were made of cotton wool and the baby mountains were like something from a chocolate box cover, a friendly place in a children's story. For a second it didn't seem real for it was all in miniature and it was exquisite and precise and modest. I realised that I am one of those people that cannot shake off the effects of what is called jet lag with its feeling of fatigue and the mind does wander.

The rooms in the hotel were, as was the case with the rest of the hotel, very clean, ordered and having a utilitarian feel. There was a view through the window of my room that travel companies like to present. The hotel was high up, maybe half way up the side of a cliff or hill having quite a sheer drop down to a winding road that led around the little town below and then along the sea front and back up through hills that looked across the baby mountains. I remember the place as being idyllic - I'll mention it just the once more. It was a shame about the effects of jet lag and the inability to sleep that first night because although not marring the experience, I would have enjoyed it all the more if feeling more awake and chipper.

Whilst lying in bed, I heard the notes from a musical instrument that sounded across the whole town and area. It was a series of single notes sounding like a chime but having a childlike or simple sound to it. I wondered what it was. It sounded at definite periods of time as a clock might chime at hourly periods but I couldn't work out what it was and what with the jet lag, it was a little irritating. All the same, it had a quality that was unusual and had raised my interest. I knew that I wasn't going to get any sleep so I arose and had a walkabout. I walked down to the town and then along the sea front. I then walked up into the mist as I climbed the hills and imagining that when getting to where I was aiming for I would be engulfed in swirling mist and would have to struggle through it. Yet the mist always disappears as one reaches the destination one is aiming for. Not that I was aiming for anywhere. I came upon little areas by the side of the road where shrines were left unattended. Within the areas around the shrines were archways and little wooden bridges and people had tied little notes or objects onto trees. These were Buddhist affairs, not temples but just little clearings in the woods where symbolic relics and totemic objects rested in ancient peace and reverence. I looked at the smouldering embers that were left in a metal bowl type of thing. I hadn't seen anyone around but there must have been someone there earlier who had visited the shrine to gather thoughts of prayer and hope and all the things that people do all over the world in their different ways but all meaning the same thing. I then followed a canal that had a path by its side. It seemed to be the only way to reach the small houses built by the side of the canal. I was feeling out of place and a bit odd as the older residents stared at me. When I gave my customary nod, it wasn't met by a reciprocal gesture but a longer stare was frozen at the foreign person who ambled with such languid liberty. I noticed the size of the people. They were smaller than the city offspring with their higher protein diet. Here the old ladies had legs like brown sticks, bowed and gnarled. The sea air with its cutting wind had lined their faces to give a look of leather. Age had taken elasticity from the skin so that it sagged from eyes that had become weak yet they held a hard gaze at the symbol of that which I felt they didn't like and that symbol was encapsulated by my very self. The clothing that they wore would not be found in any fashion house in the Ginza district of Tokyo unless of course if it was packaged and designed to be so as a peasant dress style. These are people that one in the West won't see on the Japanese game shows for this is unseen Japan and these are unseen feelings and responses to what has happened to Japan. I felt that these people remember the promises and it is, I believe, in these people that the heart and pulse remains in being Japanese.

Later on I stumbled upon a curious looking little construction that drew my attention. The little building intrigued me. It was by the side of a road that was way out of town. It was built from wood having an archway with a tiny spire at the top that sheltered a small area having two facing benches allowing room for two very small adults. The inside of the little arched construction would take only two strides to walk through. There were indentations and inscriptions carved into the blue washed wood and for some reason I thought that it was to do with Norwegian sailors. It was definitely connected with those that went to sea and to me, the inscriptions looked Scandinavian. As I was trying to make sense of the words, a mechanized sound came from the top of the little edifice and a neat wooden ledge popped out of the face of the building that held a miniature glockenspiel and by mechanical workings a little beater tapped at certain bars. And there was the sound! The little chiming sound that I heard earlier on. That sound that could be heard right across town.

Now, the reader of this rambling might well assume that I am easily pleased or was bored to a point when anything would amuse me, even the most fatuous happening but let me tell you, I felt an instant excitement run through me. I did. I had stumbled upon the thing that made that sound and it came from this most odd and intriguing little creation. I wanted to know more about the building and of its history. It made me smile. It had that eccentric Germanic staidness that translated so well with the Japanese quirkiness and I saw similarities in the different cultures such as valuing order and cleanliness. Although working as a collective, there is an accommodation for the individual to express him or herself in unusual and sometimes bizarre ways. I stood next to the little construction and looked over at the woods that were opposite and then I looked across at the baby mountains, the green leaves of trees giving them a fluffy look making them appear even more cute. I looked down at the road that wound itself to the sea front and then I looked at the buildings making up the town of Matsuzaki. From where I was standing, I had a good vantage point being able to see all around and I thought about it being Saturday morning. In England it would be about one in the morning. In eight hours it would be the same time as it was now where I was standing and for a second, I confused myself with thinking about time but stopped the thoughts almost immediately. I settled on looking at the little town.

I liked the place and I imagined it existing in England. It was Saturday as I said and a town of this size would have had a football team. Although not being a top premier team, it would be a significant club in the area and whether it was a home or away game, there would be the people connected with the club and diehard fans making preparations for today's game in their own way and capacity of course. There would be the phone calls to confirm or cancel arrangements in the business side of it all, the last minute decisions, the manager of the club maybe finding out that his striker although talented on the football pitch is also proficient at drinking alcohol, sniffing powder and pulling women who are in relationships with other men and all done in known night clubs and this striker has struck again, ending up in the local police station for being in a fight and being in possession of a class A drug. The anxiety will cause a gripping sensation in the manager's chest and even though it isn't a top club, this player earns well but he's a big fish in a small pond as they say. Other clubs, the larger ones, have shown an interest in him but all have been put off by his attitude and the way that he conducts himself. And there is also another phone call being made; this one is from one of the fans to another fan, telling him that there isn't enough room in the car to take him to the game for today happens to be an away game and the person making the difficult call is sorry but the person who usually goes feels a lot better now and has decided to come after all and the man who has received the call says that it's okay but when he puts the phone down, he feels the disappointment. He had just packed his sandwiches and had planned to take along a football programme from years ago that had a funny tale in it. He had intended to show it to the others that he thought he would be travelling with and they would all have a laugh together but no, it was not to be and he looks down at the programme and it now looks out of place and redundant. But then I realised that all this wouldn't happen anyway in England as the football season was over. It was the start of summer and the World Cup would be taking place in a week or so in the country that I was in at that moment. My imagination stopped wandering and I wondered if the little town I was in even had a football team. I didn't know. This was something that I intended to ask about during my travels but I forgot.

I had another walk around the religious constructions in the woods. There still wasn't anybody about. The charms that were used for invoking spirits were basic and I felt primitive. Then I questioned myself for thinking of it as being primitive. Why did I think that? Was it because the little charms were simple and unsophisticated? Was I comparing them to large grand churches, massive buildings of substance that have been the focal point of communities having authority through the ages and a complicated system of statuses that have developed in the organisation of the Christian religion and the power and the fear? Yet, these things that I was looking at, the little offerings, although at first sight to me at any rate looked crude, were not. You see, I have never been one that had wanted to travel in search of truths. I wasn't looking for answers. I didn't have any ideas of looking at another culture's religion with hopes that I would find something and maybe find myself. This was never in my mind but the experience in that wooded area made an impression upon me. I'm not saying any great spiritual awakening. Maybe it was more sociological but all the same it stirred thoughts for rumination.

I walked down the road that led back to town, looking behind me every so often at the hills and mountains. The low clouds were holding water that added to the damp atmosphere yet the air was fresh and soft. There was and maybe still is, a little establishment that sold tea, coffee and pastries and so I went in, made my order and sat back in a flimsy chair, feeling a tired overweight man from another place which of course I was. Then I walked by the sea as it broke onto the shore. In times like these when the senses are heightened as in this case because of tiredness, one can feel nature in a more significant way as if everything is amplified and maybe out of proportion, bursting in and through itself. Maybe that is nature in its every living moment, thrusting, growing and glaring, a discharge of life being thrown ever forward and I felt that I could actually hear the sea breaking as if cracking an iron shell. The gulls seemed to be shrieking back at the roar of the sea. The clamour of the two sounds fused as one as nature's orchestra was playing its concerto to greet another phase of light which us humans call a day.

It is a long (for me it seemed to be long) and steep climb up to the hotel where I was staying. My friend and his wife would now be climbing out of their bed and getting themselves ready to come down to the large hall where breakfast would be served. The 1950's or maybe early 1960's decor fitted the feel of a place that was out of the normal run of things. The little gowns that everyone wore added to what I saw as an eccentricity and I liked it all the more because of it. The breakfast consisted of about eight dishes and for most Westerners, it might not seem particularly suitable fare for that time in the morning although I enjoyed the experience and the food. The way it was served and how it was served in traditional cutlery contributed to the Japanese feel and authenticity. The staff in that hotel and other places are gracious and polite but do not kowtow and there is a big difference. It is one that I respect. My room in the hotel that we were staying at didn't have an en-suite toilet. It had a bath and shower but one had to walk down the corridor and use a large room that was more like a public toilet having urinals and separate compartments that had big gaps under and over the shields which I must say I wasn't that enamoured with. And then to my horror when entering one of them, the sight of just a hole in the ground where one is to do one's business greeted me. I retreated from the toilet compartment with what must have been obvious terror etched on my face and a chap who was in there must have noticed this and pointed to a few other compartments at the other end of the room. I discovered to my immense relief that they were what is referred to as Western toilets. I would have preferred more privacy but there you are, that's the way of things.

On leaving the toilets, I was reminded in an almost reprimanding manner by a middle-aged man that I was wearing the shoes that I had used for walking around the hotel and there I was standing in the toilet area. The man pointed to a stack of sandals that were by

the entrance. It is the custom for one to change one's footwear when entering the toilet. This, I was later told, is a common practice in peoples' homes and in many public places the flip-flop, sandal things are provided.

As I said, the staff are efficient without having the slimy ingratiating manner that is worked at in order to gain a tip for in TLOTRS, tipping is not the done thing. I also like that custom not only because I happen to be a tight fisted miser but also because of the feeling of embarrassment. I feel that it is a practice that is at the heart of that 'haggle and hassle' culture and all that it embraces which I do not like. I prefer a society where a person is paid a proper wage for the job that he or she does and is respected for it.

Now, what I did notice and I suppose one hasn't to be that perceptive at all to notice, that there is a big different in the service one receives from a female to a male. When being served by a man, the business is quite often conducted in an abrupt although socially acceptable polite manner. When being served by a female, the service is always a lot friendlier and performed with lots of smiles, giggles and laughter that is shielded by a dainty hand at showing such a shameless outburst of emotion. I liked that to. I'm sure most men do and maybe I have to admit it to myself that it's good for my ego which gets massaged in that manner when I'm at home about as many times as the planet I live on gets visited by aliens from outer space. Of course I liked it. And what with me and my corny quips and slapstick routines of the fat man getting in a muddle; well, it evoked these very feminine characteristics which of course is part of a culturally embedded servility where women behave in such a way for men. I thought a number of times, often with a wry smile, what the most belligerent of feminists in the West would think of this. I imagined, in true stereotypical fashion of course, a female head of a department overseeing gender studies and issues in some university who would be dressed in androgynous clothing and aping clichéd masculine body language as if to prove some political point, would make of this overly excessive deferential manner. I watched the chambermaids going about their work at the hotel and when I nodded, they could barely bring themselves to reciprocate the gesture on equal terms but lowered their heads and smiled. I watched one of them run down the corridor to get some sheets from a trolley to take into a room and then she ran back again but not with great ungainly strides. It was performed in a hurried but neat fashion with the heels of her flat shoes dragging on the ground giving the whole motion a brushed swishy sound, her legs moving only from the knees down. I noticed that another chambermaid was running and I then realised that they always ran, head in place, body in a perfect line, moving in a near gliding fashion by the dainty running fashion. My mind swayed back to where I come from and to the liberated lasses that swagger around the streets where I live, clearing their noses loudly by snorting nasal mucus up one nostril at a time before spitting it out onto the pavement, fingering large ostentatious jewellery, wearing rings that are really replicas of knuckle dusters as worn by their man mates and now absorbed into a 'his and hers' range, pulling up the jogging bottoms having the trademark sports label running down the side, the tattoo needled somewhere between the small of the back and the top of the bottom just above the crack into which the stretched cord of a thong disappears, another drag on a cigarette and then to clear the chest by coughing up a ball of bronchial fluid that is also spat onto the pavement with impunity. I know that would be a gross and absurd generalisation to hang that image on all the ladies who reside where I come from but and unfortunately it is a big but, there are many of them and even the more professional female members of society have adopted a slovenly and aggressive mode of conduct as their choice of presentation.

I'm not advocating a situation where women are secondary in any way at all or to be weak and humble in their subservience to men and being mindful to one's duty and compliant in all ways to the demands of men in a society that is run by men. I think all people should be treated fairly but there are differences. For the sake of retaining character and individuality, they should be accepted and respected.

So where was I? That's right. Watching the women who worked in the hotel looking coy as they glided along the corridor. The daintiness in the feminine presentation of manners is exhibited in many ways. When in a shop and buying a basic thing, the female assistant will often give concentrated care and attention to detail in the wrapping of the item one has bought. This presentation of feminine conduct is shown throughout the social milieu. There is the Geisha personifying a tradition where the detailed feminine characteristics are articulated assiduously and although being seen as out of time, I feel still has an influence all the same. It plays an important part through the hidden layers making up the psyche and thus being evident in everyday situations in Japanese society.

The hotel we stayed in didn't have a bar but sold beer in vending machines. Machines play a big part in Japan. I was introduced to a chair that gave one a massage. One could buy little gifts in the hotel shop but there was not much else in the way of activities to occupy and amuse guests because the place was about the hot baths. There were many places in the hotel to just sit around and read, relax, talk and generally unwind. The hotel had a 10:00pm curfew and that was it. If one went out, one had better get back before ten in the evening or one will find oneself locked out and that was the end of the matter.

We were there for two nights. The first night we stayed in the hotel and the second night we ventured out to the little town at the bottom of the steep hill or cliff that the hotel was built on. We followed the narrow path that twisted downwards to the town. The vegetation was lush and me being the absolute coward that I am, asked my friend if there were any snakes around. I was relieved and surprised to hear that there wasn't and that there weren't any snakes to be bothered about in Japan. I thought there would have been. I wasn't sure why but what with the humid atmosphere and it being foreign, I imagined that there were poisonous creatures waiting to bite into Mr Jumbo as he went about on his holiday.

I was told that the bars I would be interested in have red lanterns hanging outside of them; not to indicate that a lady of the night was operating a business in the premises but a sign denoting it as a locals' bar, a place run by the owner and not being part of some chain, a bar where the ordinary people go, bus drivers, tax collectors, policemen, bricklayers, motor cycle mechanics, people just wanting value for their yen when going for a drink and chat with others or of course by themselves. Matsuzaki is a pretty little town. I liked the feel as I liked the feel in most of the places that I went to. It has the seaside character and a quality that I felt relaxed in although it reminded me of a small coastal town somewhere in the USA, maybe in California or maybe Florida. I think it was because it had a new feel to it meaning the roads and buildings - it was the USA in miniature, the colony maybe. "Strange," I thought to myself. I hadn't reckoned with having thoughts of comparing Japan to The Land of the Rising Uncle Sam but it was there, in my mind and, dear reader, it didn't go away.

We went to a little bar that was like many local bars in Japan, having the sliding wooden screened door, stools up against the bar, small tables with stools or benches, a dark interior, little ornate light shades and a lively yet relaxed atmosphere. Basic food is prepared behind the bar, some of it cooked on little trays and a selection of tit bits to have with one's drink. There is usually music being played but not obtrusively loud. I had a beer, a large one, in fact 'jumbo' size. My friend explained the etiquette and way of things to me and I tried some of the food with their different tastes that I was told were met with abhorrence by most Western visitors but I found them to be quite nice.

So I sat there, in this little bar. I was at ease. This is what I had come to Japan for. I looked at my surroundings. They were different from what I normally see, the little bar itself, the tone and pitch of the voices coming from the people around me, the dress, in fact the dress my friend was wearing because he had come out wearing the clothes worn in the hotel, the little robe and the wooden flip-flop sandals. There were the smells and not for the first time, I was conscious of the homogeneity of race when looking at the people. I looked out of the window, the sea lay at peace, things seemed in order, in their place and everything making up the whole. I thought of Jumbo, being obviously different but I was playing my part as was everyone and everything else. Two women came in who were heavily made up and dressed in silken costumes. They were attractive but maybe overly so. For one moment I thought that they were a top draw drag act and I pointed this out to my friend who is a font of knowledge on things Japanese. He told me that the ladies were not Japanese but almost certainly Korean. I thought back to my observations a minute before of thinking that everybody was the same race and here were two ladies coming from another country but then they had similar or that's how it looked to me, physical characteristics. Maybe they shared the same origins as the Japanese. The two ladies stood at the counter for a few seconds and then turned and walked towards the end of the bar, pulled a curtain to one side and exited, going into another room or bar. My friend told me that the women were probably prostitutes. This surprised me. There I was ruminating on all things being pleasant and in harmony and a couple of women come in and remind me that things are the same everywhere and business is business but that is the way of things. Why should it surprise me? It was just that it was unexpected. Call me naive, go on, call me naive, for that is what I am in many areas of this thing that we call life.

A young man entered and looked at every face in the bar, not that there were many to look at. He took a double look at me. His gaze settling for a long instant as he took in the body and being of the bulky foreigner and then he too walked towards the curtain at the end of the bar, rolling his shoulders and swaying his body in that young man 'bursting in the cannon's mouth' manner. I watched his machismo walk which I believe is actually an outward show of behaviour that contradicts a feeling of being scared and so acts as a shield that says, "I am ready to attack." I thought that this was the first time since being in TLOTRS that I had seen geezer behaviour, meaning the hard man stance and presentation. He was holding a slim case that held a pool cue. I watched his stocky frame and the back of his shaved broad head as he pulled the curtain across and just as he went to enter the other room, I saw that there were others in there standing around a pool table and then he disappeared with the thick curtain falling in place behind him.

I wanted to go into the room but my friend's wife didn't think it would be a good idea. "Yakuza," she said and my friend confirmed this telling me that the young man was almost certainly part of a faction making up the regional Yakuza. He went on to explain of how the Yakuza operate, even in the small places; of how they supply women for business men in the Karaoke lounges where the prices are ludicrously expensive, for the drinks I mean. He told me of the rackets that the Yakuza are involved in and of how it all fits together. They aren't just the 'Johnny Rebel' type or the murky underground criminal, they are also established in all parts of Japanese culture. I sat back and pondered this. I thought of the society that has symbols reflecting the maintenance of their culture. Those symbols, images and characteristics that are understood as being very Japanese. The need and desire to conceal was a thought that recurred to me. The use of physical disguises and masks, along with all the different set of ways and customs. All performing a function of sociologistic maintenance having great strength and influence yet represented in some cases with an almost fragile representation of polite manners and make up that has been carefully applied to the face with pain staking patience and a hard earned skill coming from tradition. I thought about the stocky young man who had just entered the bar with his pool cue and I thought about the Japanese way of things. I was becoming aware that one has to guess at an inference that isn't said for the standpoint of the person is revealed between the lines and it is when reading there that one acquires the intentions, belief and opinion of the other. It is the way of not committing one's self that gives an impression of being non-confrontational and to display in public a neutrality and acquiesce to authority. Many Westerners can be infuriated to encounter people who are seen as colourless, blindly obedient, seemingly without personal opinion and always presenting compliance to order. But maybe the western observer is wrong – even deluded in believing they have a menu that offers them many cultural choices and options, for it is in the wily art form that courses through tradition, embedded in that heritage there exists an essence that has been of paramount importance for the survival of being Japanese. That is concealment and that concealment is revealed in many areas as those essential disguises that perform the function of maintenance, strength and an identity of being Japanese.

A culture of secrecy. I thought about it. The mask, the veil, disguises, camouflage, hidden and although subliminal being the foundation from which emanates the spirit that drives the whole thing. And there are the Yakuza. Gangsters yet they have a functional form within the machinery of society, contradictory on the surface because of being law breakers in a law abiding society but the central purpose is to have a society that is orderly and obedient and the Yakuza perform a role that is positive in contributing towards that society. They have been accommodated even though purporting themselves to be outsiders. They are after all a group that has order within itself and contributes towards the functioning of society in that which they operate for it is a society where people look at the group and sociologistic interests before oneself because such inappropriate behaviour and thought is reproachable and can be seen as selfishly slothful, as exaggerated in the decadent behaviour from weaker people in other societies. It is because the Yakuza isn't a lone person outside of the order of things and the individuals in the Yakuza belong to an established group having claims of ancestry and possessing Samurai qualities to substantiate their outsider status. They aren't outsiders at all but in fact yet another example of how the Japanese culture absorbs and utilises to maintain itself. Their practices are illegal and they are made up of those who aren't Japanese. Many are from Korean origin. Gambling, prostitution and corporate crime are their areas but then, fraud, deceit and corruption form the basis for all societies. What the hell would politicians do if it were otherwise?

I went up to the bar and went through my clowning routine of ordering a round of beer in Japanese, much to the amusement of the owner of the little establishment and his wife but then, she might have been the owner. It was fun and it was pleasant and relaxed. The music tinkered harmlessly, the atmosphere was cordial, the large foreigner was making light entertainment, all was in accord; and in the other room, behind a curtain, were young men who were part of a firm of gangsters and there were Korean ladies with their faces plastered in make up who were dressed in silk but they were a different kind of Gladys from their sisters who are called Geishas. They were ready to be hired out at an hourly rate to Japanese men and waited in a bar where they watched pools balls roll across a perfectly balanced surface. The elderly middle-aged woman behind the bar fizzled a giggling charm at my lumbering behaviour and I looked into her painted face, at the shine in her dark eyes. I tried to look deeply into them. Everything was fine, everything was in its place and I nodded as I turned from the bar, smiling my gratitude at the graciousness of it all. Everything was okay, everything was safe and I smiled. I sat down and we toasted Japan. I made toasts to biiru and then to draught beer which is nama biiru. It's what I preferred and it's cheaper. We toasted bullet trains, Sumo wrestlers, Mount Fuji, Geisha girls, bento boxes and we chinked glasses as we toasted the Yakuza and I thought that Mishima deserved a glass to be raised, if nothing else but for his notoriety and all things Japanese were to be celebrated. I liked the place, I had been there four or so days and already I knew that I would like to travel around the country. I would enjoy the safety, the substance and quirky character that Japan offers. If I could speak the language, it would have made it even better. As we sat around our table, the curtain to the other bar opened and a face looked right at us. It was one of the young men who was playing pool. The curtain dropped and then opened again as two young men emerged and walked towards us. One of them was carrying a camera. They stood at our table and gave the customary nod. I nodded back, noticing both of them had the tell-tale dents and scars notched into different pats of their heads and faces, the universal sign of men who have invested a lot of their time in the act of physical confrontation. I have to say I can't remember if they had the severed digits.

I looked at the camera that one of the young men was holding and I know this makes me sound stupid but it was at that moment that I thought about Japan and its relationship with cameras. I looked down at the camera that I had brought with me. Whilst making my preparations for my trip to Japan, I bought myself a throw-away camera in one of the

Chapter Six

Tesco mega stores. It had the company's colours printed onto a strip of thin cardboard running around it, the distinctive symbol of it being a cheap product, in fact the lowest price range that is advertised as being of value. I looked from the compact piece of engineering that the young man was holding back down to my flimsy looking contraption and I smiled inwardly at how bizarre it looked and that maybe these young men might think that it was an example of modernity in engineering and invention in the United Kingdom. One of the young men pointed to the tattoos on my arms and both of them nodded. The one who had pointed made an action of wanting to have a more detailed look, of wanting to hold my arm to gain greater inspection. My friend's wife told me that he wanted to have a closer look. I told him that it's okay and offered one arm and then the other. They both smiled, looking at my tattoos a little incredulously and then looked at each other. They found the tattoos interesting and amusing. I will explain why that is, dear reader. You see, my tattoos aren't the macho representations often seen displayed on men's arms and nor are they the type that was in vogue at the time. My tattoos are of animals. There is a little bird of paradise, a small butterfly, a large face of a chimpanzee on the inside of my right forearm and on the inside of my other forearm, a tattoo of a Victorian man giving a baby elephant a piggy back. They seemed fascinated, not for any length of time but just for a few moments, by the chimpanzee and elephant tattoos. They stepped back and had a look at me, searching for clues as to my social standing and then one of them patted my shoulder in a gesture that said I was accepted and all is okay. They both grinned and in a culture like Japan's giving a stranger and especially a foreigner, a playful slap on the shoulder is very unusual. But I didn't mind. I'm a broad church in that I have known and mixed with a diverse range of people in my life. We shook hands and of course their handshakes were near bone crunching. The action of shaking hands gives certain people an opportunity to demonstrate their strength by gripping the other person's hand as hard as they can and in some cases is done as a warning.

The young man showed me his camera in a gesture that asked if I would mind them taking photographs. We all had our photographs taken together. I struck the customary pose of the man in pub by giving the thumbs up gesture and this was reciprocated by the young men who came from a land where the two fingered peace sign seems to be the predominant pose when a camera is produced. I then picked up my camera from the table and the young men watched this very carefully as if I held in my hand an unknown species of small animal. I joked that it was a highly sought after piece of equipment and was too expensive to make it commonly available. This made them laugh and one of them asked if he could examine it. I handed it to him and he turned it carefully in his hands, being watched by his friend who had an expression that was mixed with being serious, puzzled and polite in not laughing. He gave the camera back to me. I pointed it at them and pressed the button and instead of the severe electronic and mechanical synchronised clicking of a shutter, a single and feeble ping sounded. Compared to the piece of engineering they had, it looked ridiculous more than just cheap.

One of the young men insisted on buying me a beer which of course I accepted. He didn't have to insist too strongly. And off they went, rolling shoulders, a swaggering lazy walk. They pulled back the curtain, enough for me to catch a quick glimpse of part of a pool table and the lower half of one of the ornately presented women and then they were gone, the curtain dropping into place hiding the other Japan but it was really part of the Japan.

I don't want to labour the subject of jet lag with its draining effects and the inability to sleep properly but I cursed myself for not being prepared and bringing some sleeping tablets with me which was something that I did on my second trip. The baths in the hotel were open all night and that's where I spent a lot of time during the dark hours. I'm not the type of person that would normally go to things like baths but I enjoyed the experience and very much so. Maybe if the whole thing was in the UK, I would have felt differently about it. In fact I don't need any time to think about that because I know it would be. The culture is different and I didn't have the self-conscious feelings because of being an alien and all that it entails in being separate and not belonging to what's going on. It was good to reside behind the protective shield of the other in knowing or feeling that one is just accepted because of the obvious difference. There were baths inside and outside. It is a relaxing experience to sit back on the rocks in the bath outside. The temperature was chilly but the hot water kept one warm whilst looking at the silhouettes of the mountains and hills. The Japanese have this cleanliness thing to a point where it's in a different orbit to what I'm used to. One has to have a shower before entering the baths and the shower can be an elaborate affair with the different soaps on offer that are used for cleaning oneself. Thick lathers are made as one soaps oneself and then a considerable time is taken in showering before actually getting into a bath which is a communal affair as it is shared with other people. It could be a dozen people or maybe just a few others lounging in the water. On entering the area, one is supplied with a little square of white cloth which I thought was used to cover oneself in an act of modesty but no, they use them to apply the soapy lather to their bodies whilst showering and when finishing with the shower, they get into the bath, settle themselves and fold or roll the little cloth into a neat shape before placing it on their heads.

In many places one has to cover tattoos as they are seen as being a sign of criminality but in the hotel where we were staying, there wasn't a requirement for me to cover mine. Tattoos are associated with the Yakuza and in Japanese fashion the custom to cover, hide and conceal also includes the indelible ink that is needled into one's skin. I went to a gym that had a swimming pool on my first trip. My friend was a member and although I can't swim I went in the pool but was told that I had to cover my tattoos and was given adhesive tape. I don't know if the practice has slackened as the fashion for tattoos has now extended into many areas of society. One will now see female art school students exhibiting tattoos and the inky illustrations are seen on the bodies of pop musicians and the like. But, there it was and as I entered the bath in the hotel, wearing nothing but holding the little white cloth, a man approached me from the side. He too was naked except for the black rimmed glasses that he wore and he nodded slightly in an act of almost polite reverence as he caught my attention and he said, "Excuse me, sir, excuse me but are you - fooligan?"

I explained to him that I wasn't. It must have looked an absurdly stupid scene, what with me attempting to convey that I wasn't a football thug and neither of us understood each other's language. It wasn't the only occasion that my appearance was noticed and I suppose that I would be noticed. Things were said about me in the knowledge that I couldn't understand what was being said but from the way the eyes studied and judgments were made, I didn't have to understand verbal communication to know that remarks were being made about me. And yet, although there were the grilling looks and the rudeness of obviously talking about me, I didn't care because it was as if it didn't matter anyway as I wasn't part of the whole thing.

I enjoyed my stay at the Onsen and on the Sunday afternoon my friend, his wife and myself took the bus and train back to Isehara. It was a good train having seats that were positioned sideways giving the passenger a view out of the window. I had been on a similar kind of train in the USA. It was a holiday weekend in Japan and the Japanese spill out of the congested cities and travel to the open spaces making the most of a break. I gave up my seat to a woman so that she could sit with a few of her friends on the 'viewing' seat. She was polite and nodded many times at me and I also nodded because I wanted to be friendly and I liked the feel of things. I looked out of the window as the train traced its way around the coastline and every now and then the sea would appear. I looked down at the woman and she smiled and nodded some more and I smiled and looked out of the window. "Friendly person," I thought to myself and she didn't ask if I was a fooligan.

* * * * * * * * *

All that happened the year before and here I was on my second trip, sitting on the station platform with a bento box waiting to catch a bullet train that would take me south. I was excited about getting on a bullet train. I like trains and always have done. I've mentioned train spotting before and of how it is often regarded as a hobby and interest that is ridiculed and that the people who participate in the pursuit of collecting train numbers are often individuals that are mocked and lack any credit by many who strive for social acceptance in mainstream culture. But I've always liked trains and I thought about this as I waited and watched a bullet train pull into the station onto the opposite track. The white line of carriages rolled perfectly on the continuous railed track that is bedded on what looked to be a modern foundation of stones and white concrete sleepers. The magnificent front of the train leads the way although it can also be an eerie sight, something of a monster-like insect creature with its protruding nose. There is a slit for the driver to look out of and beneath the slit are two lights that are the eyes of the sinister looking metal creation. I couldn't make out a mouth. The train rolled to a stop and I surveyed the outstanding spectacle of engineering. It was a wondrous mechanical beast indeed. This was the first time that I had had a good look at a bullet train having seen them on my first trip but not having the opportunity to pay close attention to their detail. Watching the train caused me to become excited. I was really looking forward to getting on one. The long train opposite me silently moved its perfectly balanced self until it was at quite a speed before I realised

that it was moving and then away from the station it rolled, barely audible. Further it travelled into a distance that probably looked pretty much the same as it did where I was sitting and it went down a precise and near faultlessly straight track and it didn't jolt from side to side because it ran on a continuously welded rail.

I checked the lights at the end of the platform, waiting for them to change colour and thus signal the imminent arrival of the bullet train that I would be catching. When the train did arrive, I felt a similar feeling to what some might feel when boarding an aeroplane. I suppose because it wasn't a common experience for me, there is something special about the bullet train that gives one a sense of partaking in a higher level of travel. All seats face in the same direction. I chose my seat and settled myself, looking at the people around me. They all looked Japanese, mostly business types and then I looked out of the window. I wasn't aware that the train had already started to roll, moving in a heavy silent motion as smooth as velvet and as powerful as a rocket breaking out of the Earth's atmosphere. This gimpy anorak of a foreigner was letting his imagination run away with itself. I watched a small light that flickered on a map at the end of the carriage, marking where we were on our journey. I was heading to the city called Hiroshima which, along with the city Nagasaki, for an obvious reason symbolises a distinctive landmark in the level of atrocity that humans inflict upon one another. About twenty minutes or so later out of the window to my right was a vision of another magnitude but this one being the magnificent Mount Fuji. Although it stood many miles in the distance the snow capped wonder showed its powerful presence and I felt that even the engineering marvel that is the bullet train bowed its long nosed head in reverence to the natural geographical brilliance that has held humans in awe and has been worshipped in TLOTRS for thousands of years.

I ordered a cup of coffee from the young lady who was doing the rounds with the trolley; not because I wanted one but just so I could absorb the whole experience and to be served by the charming young lady. Just as a schoolboy might do, I placed the coffee on the little fold down table in front of me and watched it. The coffee did not spill or even stir because the Shinkansen, known as the bullet train is a marvel of engineering endeavour. We were moving at two hundred and eighty five kilometres per hour yet having a feeling of being motionless. I looked around my fellow passengers. They were high-tech people in suits and then I looked out of the window. The urban debris was now gone and the land was flat and spreading out as far as I could see. It looked like glass but the sheen is water lying on flat land that is growing rice and a man was riding a bicycle down a little track running between the great fields, a hat on his head, trousers that went down to only just beneath his knees, looking like he is dressed from another land. Parts of his attire are now worn by younger people in their casual leisurewear pursuits as peasant meets post-modern but he is in work that contributes to the essential foundation of this mighty land. Rice is much more than just a common product for business people to quantify when deriving optional prices in utilities or something that is given a lesser thought of being common food in a take-away restaurant late at night because rice is symbolic to survival. During the time of the second World War, there was a practice of shining one grain of rice individually by the suffering residents in a battered Tokyo. There was still dignity and the polishing of the rice was a discipline. It showed pride and the importance that was given to the seemingly humble and inconsequential grain of rice. No, it means far more than just a basic food and although in comparison a grain of rice appears meagre to the grand power of technological advances and economical exchange mechanisms, it is part of the bedrock, staple in diet to the physical and mental being for the people who come from TLOTRS.

The small red light flickered on the map at the far end of the carriage indicating that we had moved along a little more. I sat back, basking in it all. I could feel the pride associated with the Shinkansen. I had read that the Japanese were the first to build railway lines to accommodate super speed trains. "The marvel of it all," I kept thinking to myself. I thought of the preciseness in the engineering and the running of the train system. To be on time, the indicators show you where to stand on the platform so that you're in the correct place to board your carriage and I started to think of the staff working on the train system, of their conduct and stature in Japanese society. These were thoughts that I would return to during my visit.

And again I looked around at the other people in the carriage. There was no shouting, nobody talked into mobile phones with impunity and so being inconsiderate to other people who have to share the confined space. Shoes were removed before placing one's feet on the seat; this is a practice that I value. I know I might sound a bit cranky to place importance on this social etiquette yet I believe it is worth taking note of when considering social manners and observing that standards of behaviour have slipped. There apparently seems to be an acceptance to the rise in aggressive and violent conduct. The act of removing one's shoes shows a respect for public property and for other people who share it with you; in short, it isn't selfish to do so. Whilst it is to place one's shoes on the opposite seat or to fold one's legs beneath oneself without removing one's shoes that have carried one around streets, treading in all kinds of stuff and then to smear it on the seat. The words 'consideration' and 'respect' stand opposed to the prevalent conduct where the words 'arrogance' and 'bullying' hold sway as the ways of the coward have found endorsement. And yes, I stand by my opinion of placing shoed feet on seats as an indicative symbol of sociologistic attitudes; even be it one small act. As a child, as was the case for many others, I wouldn't have thought of doing such a thing in a public place. My mum would have admonished me immediately, letting me know in no uncertain terms why I shouldn't do such a thing. I was told of 'good manners' and that term encompassed everything to do with everything even as I have thought in later years, if it allowed others to act badly against me. It doesn't matter what social standing a person has or what type of family or background one might come from, good manners was the motto and especially to be adopted if coming from a poorer background. What one might lack in material terms, one can make up in personal virtue. As the saying goes, 'good manners cost nothing'.

I remember whilst once travelling on an inter city train observing how a young lady plonked her feet on the seat opposite her. There she was dressed in the uniformed student look, reading an academic novel. By the title on the cover, I would say a course book that had to be read. In later life she might occupy a position of authority in society and thirty years ago she wouldn't have slumped in the seat and put her feet up on the seat. She caught me looking at her and I immediately looked away. I would have liked to have said something like, "You seem to be a pleasant person, doing your education, probably seeing yourself as reasonably intelligent, having an understating of intellectual debate – don't you think that by shoving your dirty shoes on the seat doesn't take into consideration other people; like maybe, a woman who might be wearing a nice dress or a man going to an interview". She gave a look that said I was the bad man and I knew, what with my bulky presentation, that I would be seen as the thug, the aggressor because she can fit the type of the nice and sensitive young woman doing her studies, minding her own business and who's this intruding into her bubble of a worldly existence? Well, if it's not an aging skinhead, that old enemy of the sophisticated classes. Yes, it's the fooligan.

Another example happened a few years back during the course of my work. I attended meetings where men and women who revelled in having and reminding others that they had a qualified status in their jobs. These people worked in the field of community nursing and social work and there were those having occupations called psychologists. I would watch as some of them would breeze into a room, plump themselves down in a chair with their feet or foot under their body. On one occasion I said to a social worker, a man of about forty odd years of age, that didn't he think it bad manners to put his feet on the chair considering that the chair was quite new and the fabric on the chair cover was light. The man didn't answer me but just looked at me. I had said it quietly. Nobody else heard and I said it in what I believed to be a friendly manner. But this man didn't like it. He continued to look at me and I then looked more closely at him, at what he was wearing and I considered the type of person that he was. This man didn't have a leather briefcase to hold his documents and files but a shoulder bag that one might have taken as an accessory to a rock concert many years ago. It was made of rough fabric in a designed army fatigue kind of thing. He had a crew cut haircut but having a wisp at the back with a small bead secured onto it and then his eyes narrowed and in an arrogant tone of voice he asked me what job I did. Now, even though this man was in paid conventional employment working with the straights, he wore clothes that came from a counter culture that intended to rebel against the institutions and structures that this man was now part of. The only remnant of rebellion he indulged in was to put his feet on the chairs, probably because they weren't his. But the point I am attempting make here is that the man didn't like what I had said to him. I saw his attitude as selfish. He saw mine as possibly threatening and coming from a culture he felt an aversion towards.

Like many others I have not so much been shocked but dismayed at this tumble down of standards. There is the fad for the informal and casual in our society where the individual has been given a principal concern. This can be seen to have led to the self itself having taken precedence over all matters in a so called progressive culture where self analysis has become the norm and the process of typification for purposes of measurement has generated an industry that self-perpetuates labelled beings denoting a worth and value. Some more than others are judged as commanding respect and God help those who haven't been included in a group of perceived worth because it seems no-one else will. I will finish this particular tirade with an example of when I was in a library that is local to where I live. I was at a table trying to concentrate as I was writing something and a young child, maybe no older than five or six years of age, kept running up and down the aisle of books next to me. The young child was pulling at books and giving shrieking noises whilst her mother idly passed the time browsing through books on the shelf. I said to the woman in a quiet tone and making a point to be pleasant, "Excuse me but I'm trying to concentrate here on something that is important to me – I was just wondering if she," and I nodded my head at the little girl who was running along the aisle and shouting, "you know, could..." The woman looked at me and did not look down once at her child. She then turned and said, "Come on darling, come away from the nasty man, there's a good girl." See? Now don't start me.

I let the memory fade down the long carriage of the bullet train, relaxing in my seat, comfortable that I was out of reach from that behaviour, savouring the manners and propriety that was around me. But then the Japanese aren't always that considerate and courteous themselves when it comes to leaving young girls and women alone as they make their way to work, school or wherever it might be that they're travelling to. No, because I have read that there are women only carriages during busy times on weekdays in the urban areas. The carriages are demarcated by symbols in a pink colour and pink signs indicate where to stand on the platform in order to board the women only carriage giving women and girls a haven from the lecherous men who have a habit of rubbing themselves against them and 'feeling them up' as they say. Again, I thought to myself, that an accommodation is made in this society for behaviour even though that behaviour is horrible and must be illegal.

I looked up at the map with the red dot of light marking our progress. We had already stopped at Nagoya and we had also stopped at Kyoto and Osaka as we carried on travelling south. We came into a station and I saw that we had arrived at Kobe – this was a fast way to travel. I looked at the architecture outside the window. It was pretty much the same as everywhere else in the big town way of things, grey concrete and steel with plenty of glass. That drowsy feeling that comes over you when on a train fell upon me. I liked the feeling and settled in my seat, watching people leave and enter the train and again I absorbed the luxury of it all. I fell in and out of the land of slumber, a place of rushing faces, thoughts and voices, coming in a distorted form, fragmented and often surreal but I didn't slip in too deep, submerging only for short lapses, enough for the red light to have moved along the map. There was a man in a uniform looking down at me. He was checking the tickets. He took his job seriously, wearing his uniform with pride, his presentation was smart, clean, having attention to detail, the micro-embodiment of a successfully functioning society of which he was a representative. Around his body, hanging, hooked and pinned onto different parts of his uniform were the accoutrements needed to perform his work effectively. I showed him the rail pass and he studied it before handing it back to me. I said, "Thank you." He grunted something that sounded like, "Hike." This man could give orders. It was in his deportment and again I thought of the railway staff and of how they are sticklers for the rules but their official manner can have a soft edge. It is often the way in Japan to direct through suggestion rather than commit oneself to confrontational acts.

I smiled to myself as I remembered how earlier in the week I had taken the train into Tokyo, had a browse around and then took a train out again, heading for the coast. It was a small line and I wasn't really sure where I was going. What made me smile was the fact that I was two faced as is nearly everybody else on this planet because there I am, going on about the benefit of law and order and people being honest towards each other and all that and I was trying to avoid paying part of my fare. The reason why I embarked on this fraudulent path was because of the difficulty there is of buying a ticket that allows one to travel on one line and to buy another ticket to travel on another line that is owned by a different company and it was further complicated because of the language thing. So, I boarded the train from a station in central Tokyo, knowing that I didn't have the correct ticket. Remember that the rail pass that I had bought before coming to Japan was only valid on certain lines, the ones that the bullet trains operated on of course but I must admit that I was confused by the system. Anyway, the train hugged a pleasant piece of coastline before eventually pulling into a quiet little station. I stepped off the train with a handful of people who were neat and pleasant looking, just like the area. As we made our way to leave the rural little station, I made a mistake in my crime by making too much of a show of being the lost portly foreigner and it caught the attention of a well meaning lady who had also stepped off the train. In her act of courtesy and gentle self-effacement she tried to explain to me that my ticket wasn't valid. And then Mr Ticket Collector appeared, probably having heard what was going on and made an appearance from his office. This station was a one-man affair and although not far from Tokyo, it was countryside pace and as he had all the time in the world, he also had the time to check the details of my ticket. He looked at it and smiled an apology, telling me that I didn't have the correct ticket and that it wasn't valid for travel on that particular line. I made out that I didn't understand what was going on and then he did something that stopped my act and gave me an interesting insight into the Japanese way of things. This man wasn't going to accuse me of being a liar and attempting to avoid payment, God forbid. I was an honest citizen but one who had inadvertently made a mistake and as I had learned from the year before when getting to the airport on the wrong day, if it is an honest mistake, then it is accepted. And this is how it was dealt with. Mr Unknowing Well Padded Foreigner was told that he couldn't get off at that station but had to return to where he had come from and buy the correct ticket that allows him to do so.

See? There is no accusation of attempted fraud. There is no confrontation. It is the way of things. He smiled at me because everything was now understood and resolved. And the pleasant woman who had come to my aid who was dressed in a precise and daintily decorated lemon coloured dress suit? Well, she nodded and smiled now that I wasn't confused anymore and she waved as she left the station with her two friends who like her, were carrying bags from clothes stores, undoubtedly having been on a shopping trip to Tokyo and having the correct tickets, of course. I looked into the face of the station man. I didn't try it on, not even in an half hearted way. It wasn't worth it. He was unmovable in his duty. I looked into his eyes. They gave nothing away even if he knew Mr Stupid Foreigner was trying it on.

An Unlikely Fooligan

I sat back in my seat. The bullet train was speeding south and I smiled some more as I thought of my failed attempt earlier in the week. I watched the red dot flash our current position on the map for Master Shinkansen doesn't pause for breath as wheels move on a steel rail that is attached to the Earth that is moving and everything is moving and tilting at great speed in a place somewhere that we try to make sense of. And I breathed deeply, breaking out of the mode of thought that was descending upon me in a warm wave. I shifted in my seat and took out my wallet. I checked what money I had and the bits and pieces that I had accumulated that take up room in one's wallet. There was a business card that I had kept from my trip the previous year. On one side of the card, there was Japanese writing which meant nothing to me and on the other side was the name and title of a man. The card read, ITSUO YOSHINO, Mayor, HIRATSUKA-CITY and there was also the address. Whilst staying with my friend the previous year, I had decided to have a day trip and wanted to look out to sea. My friend told me of a place that wasn't that far away and could be reached by catching just one bus. I liked the idea of this, getting a bus from the local station that would probably be guided out by one of the senior citizens giving directions with one of those sticks having a light on the end. My friend gave me directions of how to travel from Isehara to Hiratsuka which is a small town on the coast lying directly south from Isehara, just west from Tokyo; so off I went with my trusted phrase book.

My friend had told me the number of the bus that I needed and after a bit of confusion trying to find the correct stand to catch it, I was soon on my way. The driver looked at me. He nodded and smiled and I smiled back. Remember, the World Cup was starting the following week and this driver had been, as had millions of Japanese people, subjected to the all pervading media hype with its depiction of English football fans being thugs and it had instilled an expectation of trouble and now that the foreign intrusion was imminent, it had ignited a vigilance and fixed to the fore of the imagination was the embodiment of this threat – the fooligan himself. The driver and I exchanged a few more nods and I expected him to say something about football, maybe the seemingly ubiquitous name 'Beckham' but he didn't. He drew his attention to looking out front, the wheels began to roll and he gave a quick look over his right shoulder and then looked to the front again, settling himself as the bus chugged carefully out of the station area. I noticed that there wasn't an elderly citizen with his warning stick giving guidance. Sometimes they give a sanctification as the vehicle moves away, set in Shinto psyche, pointing a finger in the direction that the vehicle was going, the 'way'. I had seen it done a few times by the older people and the train drivers themselves as if giving a blessing.

The bus reached the terminus at Hiratsuka town centre which is a good walk from the sea front but was on that side of the town so I didn't have to walk through the centre itself. I remember it as being a sunny day, blowing a wind in that seaside breezy way and I negotiated my way to the seafront with aid of my trusted phrase book. I like seaside towns and Hiratsuka, for me, had the feel of a seaside town back in Blighty. It was clean, of course. It had those little seaside shops selling cheap crafts and objects only seen in seaside towns. There was an ice cream shop although not the congestion of chip shops. There was the 'treat' food that youngsters have and are told will ruin their tea or dinner or supper. Anyway, I had a saunter along the front and rested on the shore, loafing and watching people go about their lives and I don't know why but I was mildly surprised to see a group of young people with surfboards. The shore came up to a concrete road and I walked along looking at the small houses that lined it and faced out to sea. I have always thought when looking at places where people live next to the sea, that their lives are different from the people who pass by them; the day-trippers like me. I have sometimes thought that they have some maritime connection and I would look into the windows to see if there was any evidence of this. It was as if because they lived by the sea, a place associated with leisure, I thought that they didn't do the normal things that people did, meaning all the people that didn't live next to the sea.

I have thought that maybe a lot of people who live in little houses facing out to sea are retired. Some might go out on the life-boat and there are those who make a living from fishing or have jobs on the ferries that glide through the sea but then maybe some of them work on the big ships, like the huge flat looking tankers that can be seen in the distance as if lying dormant in the sea. Although in reality I suppose they are like people who live anywhere, only a few would be working locally, selling knick-knacks and ice cream or having anything to do with the sea. Their lives were the same except for the view that they had and maybe being more conscious of the weather and the threat of flooding.

I walked by the side of the houses. They were small and as I often thought whilst on my visit in TLOTRS, they seemed flimsy and insubstantial, like prefabricated buildings rather than solid brick constructions. Electrical wires were visible on the outside and there were gas bottles. It had a transient feel about it. I had noticed this elsewhere even in the cities. I had been told it was due to Japan having earthquakes that a culture of building homes had evolved where there was an acceptance that it might not be there tomorrow. It made me think of the ever evolving and readiness to adapt that is very much part of Japanese outlook, an important part of their success in remaining autonomous and gaining achievements that are revered by others. Although it did seem to be a paradox, here I was in a country that has been described as one of the most advanced countries on Earth, in some fields that is and yet many people live in what would be judged as inferior housing by those living in countries having so called advanced economies. The country had a good education I was told, above that compared to where I come from. Health, housing and all the advantages and opportunities that one expects in major countries also exists in Japan.

I took a slow saunter through the alleys and narrow tracks between the houses, noticing faces at windows staring before retracting and then from nowhere, a postman on a small motorbike came hurtling around the corner. He stopped to check the number of an address, looking around himself and after gaining his bearing, he twisted the throttle on the handlebar and he was off again. I thought that it must be confusing to find the addresses but there had to be an order of things even though to my understanding it all looked a bit jumbled.

I found my way out of the estate and walked up a wide concrete avenue that took me back to town and as I walked, I was conscious of being gawped at by some people. Heads turned in cars. As people passed, their eyes fixed onto me. I knew what it was. It was the fooligan factor.

I walked into town and saw large green and white flags hanging across the high street and the other roads leading off the main thoroughfare. It took a second for me to realise that there was writing on the flags that was in English. This surprised me because of the scarcity of written English anywhere and when reading it I was taken back. On some of the flags was written, 'We welcome Eagles' and on other flags was, 'Hiratsuka Supports Nigeria'. Some of the flags were massive and all of them were green and white and of course, it dawned on me. They were the colours of the Nigerian football strip and there was the Eagle, the emblem of Nigeria boldly printed on the flags. I thought, "Why is there such a fuss about Nigeria?" The flags were everywhere and when entering the railway station concourse, I saw a cabin draped in green and white with photographs of the Nigerian team on the front and posters of the team on the side. Written on the front of the cabin was, 'Hiratsuka Supports Nigeria'. There was some Japanese writing in small letters over a large sign that read, 'Nigeria Training Site Information Centre'. Green and white scarves hung from the top, front and sides of the cabin and inside sat three people, two men and a woman wearing green shirts with whistles hanging around their necks, green ones of course. Behind them hung Nigerian football shirts in home and away colours.

The people in the cabin were elderly. They smiled as I approached them and one of the men pointed at me. "Eagles," he said, that being the name of the Nigerian football team and he pointed to the green eagle on one of the flags. "England," I said, pointing at myself in a genial manner. This caused them to giggle and shake their heads as they all said together, "Iie, iie, no." The lady looked closely at me. Leaning forward she asked in a polite way, "Are you fooligan?" I explained to them that I wasn't and that I was staying with a friend in Isehara. They had heard of Isehara but as for the rest of what I was saying, well, it was just lost in that confused maze where most communication ends up.

They gave me a small poster of the Nigerian football team and a local paper that was a special edition dealing with the World Cup and I was surprised to see that there was English writing in the paper. It showed the tables and teams and who was playing who and what teams were in the same group. Of course, Nigeria were in England's group. There was a photograph of the Nigerian team and written below in English, it said that the Nigerian team was staying in Hiratsuka. They were using the town as their base and it gave the name of the hotel that they were staying at. Standing next to the team was a Japanese man dressed in suit, smiling, in that way that politicians do. I didn't know who he was then but later on I was going to meet the man. I said farewell to the people in the kiosk, left the station area and walked into the town. The 'Eagles' were everywhere. It was a green and white outbreak of flags and bunting and children ran by me holding little green and white flags. I felt a sense of siege mentality as if my nation was under threat and here I was in a foreign land witnessing such support for what appeared as an alliance against my country. It was a strange feeling. As I walked under great billowing green and white flags, I was caught up in the squealing excitement of young Japanese school children, a disposition they normally seem to be in as it goes but now with an added exuberance. There were green and white banners boldly claiming, 'For The Victory' and 'Hiratsuka Supports Nigeria'. I turned into another street and it looked like a film set. The staged show was reaching its climax with hundreds of neatly turned out Japanese schoolchildren lining the side of the road facing the shops, waving the little green and white flags in joyous fever showing a radiance of happiness and smiles at being allowed such a treat. What was it with the whole place? This was Japan for God's sake and here they are, going full tilt in their support for one of Africa's top football teams and the one that happens to be playing England.

Camera crews negotiated for space in the crowd and then there was a high pitched scream of a roar. Although not being the tallest person, my height gave me a vantage point in that I could look over the heads of the people that crowded the side of the road, albeit that the vast majority were school children. From the front of a building which I worked out to be a hotel, walked a line of tall muscular African looking gentlemen dressed in green and white tracksuits. Children pushed forward with their bodies and teeth, each face emblazoned with a smile, waving flags at the line of self-conscious looking black men. Cameras flashed and the pitch of the screaming noise made me laugh. I noticed the different members of the Nigerian team looking at one another, a smile ready to break but not really knowing what to do.

The team walked right in front of me. I was surprised by the size and physical presence of them. I don't think it was only because I had been in a country for a week where people are generally shorter that it made them appear bigger but they were a formidable looking bunch and I immediately felt a concern for the players in the English football team, thinking that they didn't stand a chance in any physical contest with these gladiatorial athletes. I eased myself forward to the front of the crowd and I don't know why but I said very loudly to one of the passing Nigerian players in what I intended to be an English tone of voice coming from the World Service radio in the nineteen twenties, "Excuse me sir. England four, Nigeria nil." The player turned quickly on hearing my words and pointed at me and the player next to him clapped his hands and laughed. The player who had pointed at me said, "What? No way," and laughed and I smiled and they smiled and as another player passed me, he gave me a look which seemed to ask, "What the hell are you doing here?" And, "Isn't this a bit bizarre?" I raised my eyebrows and we exchanged smiles. It was all good humoured and everybody did as they were supposed to do. It went as planned. It was polite, it was safe – and then the Nigerian team were gone and the lesson was over for the school children.

An Unlikely Fooligan

The street became quiet as normal sounds resumed. It was as if it had stopped raining. The excitement of the carnival had passed. But here in Hiratsuka, there was no scattered debris of cans, bottles, paper hats and cups and all the other stuff that litters a place after an event. There were no little motorised vehicles whizzing around with a nozzle at the front sucking up discarded bits and pieces or the lorries and waste bins filled with the stuff. There was no clatter of a clean up operation because here, the school children and other people quietly disengaged themselves from their positions where they were standing and dispersed, carrying the bits of paraphernalia that they had been given and drifted back into Hiratsuka life. I walked up the road and saw a man in a suit talking to a man who was holding a microphone and the two of them were being filmed. I stood by and watched. I had nothing else or better to do. I noticed a couple of bull necked types in dark suits with a wire going into their ears standing around the area so I guessed that the man in the suit was a figure of importance. You know how certain people have this protection, like a politician or a criminal, rather than someone who had developed a way of performing brain surgery that will save millions of lives in the years to come. The film crew unfolded themselves away from the man in the suit. I stepped up to him and went through my routine of nods and smiles. He nodded back and I said, "Hi." The man gave a slight bow of his head and smiled back at me. I asked him if he spoke English and in a modest way, he told me that he spoke only a little and although his English wasn't good it was adequate to make himself clear. We spoke about the Nigerian football team staying in town and about where I come from in England. He told me that he liked London and Scotland. He told me that he was the mayor and he gave me his business card, a practice that is common in Japan. He also told me that his daughter was studying at a university in Britain and I asked if he would mind having his photo taken which he didn't. Now, this man had a few people floating around him and I gave one of them my 'use once' camera. He inspected it carefully. I then put my arm around the Mayor's shoulder and as I did this a man in a suit stepped towards us but the Mayor waved the man away without saying anything but gesturing that everything was okay and that there was no need for alarm. The man holding my camera took aim but then had difficulty in taking the photograph. After some fussing about, the button was pressed and the thin little 'ding' noise that it made sounded and the man lowered the camera and looked at it, in disbelief I thought. I shook hands with the Mayor and imparted what passes for my wit and then one of the Mayor's men stepped in front of me and took a photograph of me, so I raised my camera and took a photograph of him taking a photograph of me. The dual was one sided on the technological scale. Whilst his Canon or whatever it was, super shot deluxe made its fast whirring shutter clicking process sounds, mine responded with its 'ding' courtesy of a tiny spring that was probably glued inside the camera.

We said our farewells to each other with the Mayor telling me to call him if I needed or wanted to. Later on, I looked at the newspaper that was given to me at the station kiosk, the special with the World Cup information in it. Sure enough, there he was standing next to the Nigerian team, Itso Yoshino, Mayor of Hiratsuka, smiling, like all political types, not letting an opportunity slip, as was the world of commerce, exploiting the World Cup to promote their businesses. When I returned to Isehara, I showed my friend's wife the photograph in the paper and told her of my day's adventure. She explained to me that the mayor was quite a well known figure in the world of politics. "Oh well," I thought to myself, somewhere in his security's annals is a photograph of him standing next to a Western gentleman on the corner of the street at the time when the Nigerian football team were in town.

* * * * * * * *

That was the year before and here I was on the train entering the station in Hiroshima. I looked about the inside of the carriage, thinking of this train, the great marvel of mechanical movement that would bring overwhelming joy for George Stephenson if he could have beheld such a thing as the Shinkansen. And I thought of George Stephenson's Rocket standing alongside the Shinkansen and I thought about those Native American Indians who would have been awestruck when sighting the Iron Horse chugging across the Great Plains but if they saw this noble horse, their shields would be raised to the powers that be for giving us the opportunity to create such wonder. I'm sure that they would also pray that humans could one day have the mind to use that creativity in a more positive way for all who share nature's glory.

Seven

I alighted from the train and walked down the platform, my eyes everywhere, scanning the buildings around me and anything really that might show some evidence to what had happened in nineteen forty five. I'm sure most people, probably of a certain age, do the same. The magnitude of that occurrence has left its imprint on our psyche. As seems the case with other Japanese cities, Hiroshima looks modern with the grey and glass look, a grid road system and people who look the same as they did in the last city. I stood outside the railway station and studied my map with plans of going to the Peace Memorial Park. I asked passers-by how I could get there - with the help of my phrase book, of course. It was a bus ride and it has got to be my morbid personality I suppose but I had the event that occurred in nineteen forty five on my mind all the while. That happening that is just referred to by many Japanese people as 'the bomb'. I stood at the front of the bus looking at the faces around me, at the driver, at the young people, at the people waiting for buses on the pavement outside, at the people trying to cross the road. I suddenly became conscious of myself and where I was – there I was, the foreign man, on the bus, with a blue suitcase and a holdall bag, looking about himself, trying to take it in. The bus driver pointed out of the window towards the other side of the road where there was an opening to a large park and he nodded, letting me know that this was my stop. I stepped off the bus and looked across the wide road at the park and buildings in it. I looked around and felt the vibrating pulse that is the action of a city and thought about this place called Hiroshima, having risen from ashes and is yet another testament to human resilience.

Hiroshima Harry got harried all right – Harry monked, good and proper. I stood at the bus stop and looked across the road at what is called the Peace Memorial Park. It's in the middle of the city amongst the large stores and the side streets having bunches of small shops, outlets and services offered in a hectic retail fusion. Concrete blocks with signs told you what different shop, service or amusement was on what floor. 99.9% was unintelligible to me. It meant nothing. The pale colours of posters and streamers mixed with ringing music. It was all blasting out and the constant commentary of an urgent voice, strained and crackling from a loud speaker or hailer, presumably pushing wares and services enhanced the feeling of being an alien. I breathed into myself as if holding in the tension of the moment and then letting out my breath. As I let out my breath, a distance between my surroundings and myself deepened and continued to grow until I settled on a place that was apart but within. A feeling of stillness filled me. By looking at and considering what was around me, I was gaining a clearer insight and understanding into my own culture that lay in the sea six thousand miles away. As I looked at the people, cars and road structure of this city, I breathed in again, this time to imagine the sullied air that engulfed this area on the 6th August 1945. The city has been rebuilt but clocks and watches are still set, broken in time at 8:15am when a flash of light and tremendous sound rewrote the psychological historiography of modern Japan. I was standing in the place where it happened, dropped from the cradling arms of Enola Gay was the bomb, perversely named 'Little Boy'. It delivered its blistering kiss and a deep rupture has become established within the Japanese mind and has thus become part of the other well known attributes that are seen as Japanese. This deep and painful scar is different from the others, different from polite manners or rigid discipline. This part is of humbleness and as a wild animal has to drag an injured leg, this country has become lame. It shows it to the world for everyone to see just as a fighter in the ring gets knocked onto his back foot when a sudden explosive punch knocks him from his course and plan of action and now is wary, having to spar instead of attack, having to reassess his situation, looking at himself differently as he now has to look differently at his opponent.

I looked around myself. I felt that I had slipped into a state of disconnection and this is how I would stay for the rest of my trip.

I gained a clear and even effulgent picture and sense of the place and the people at who I was looking. One cannot help, if one is interested in people that is, to make comparisons with one's own way of life whilst being in and looking at another culture. This anthropological saunter was giving me insights into my own background and beliefs and inadvertently so just by having my wander in TLOTRS. I walked across the road to The Hiroshima Peace Memorial Museum after I was given directions from a young woman who shared with many other young people in Japan an interest in wanting to speak and try out their English. I commented on how good her English was. This I knew would please her which it did and she gave forth with a peal of little girl giggles. The museum itself presented itself as an anti-nuclear statement supported with anecdotal, drawn, photographed and filmed evidence. It is sentimental, it is true and I felt it to be numbingly futile – by coming here the course of my thoughts changed.

Inside the museum, schoolchildren in their scores moved like amoeba in twisting queues. Looking at their faces, I saw the predominant 'grinning god' coursing itself through their bodies. Holding their school project papers and ticking boxes, they were adding to the new great discourse of the country in which they were born. Some of the school children were dressed in their dark blue and white uniforms that are based on the old British navy style of uniform. I felt it to be an irony, wearing a military tunic with its short upright collar, looking more pre than past present to the films they were staring at from the nineteen forties. This country is born on discipline with purposes intended for an internal affair yet will brush against the other and take but defines its resoluteness in being in itself. The little boys were dressed in outfits that their great or great, great grandfathers would have worn when going to battle with neighbouring countries in order to expand upon the continent their way for the interests of Japan. And now the Japanese child is witnessing a depleted spirit so removed from the attitude of his or her great, great grandfather in asking for leniency and propounding humanitarian virtues yet, noticeably for me, still dressed in the uniform of skirmish.

The museum has different floors having exhibits, films and facilities that interpret and explain in different languages. Stories are told of individuals who on that day when Little

Boy came to town were going about their lives as normal. There are accounts of teachers, young children, postmen and others, their activities graphically depicted, people having had their breakfast and making their plans for later in the day after being at work or school, a child going into the back garden to wait for an older brother or sister to walk to school with – and then it happened. Thunder and Light. It is impossible for me to imagine what it was like. Did most of them know anything? Was it just, over? Or was there instant fear as the sky suddenly darkened and a roaring noise that became unbearable was forced by a crushing wind and the dust, heat and sound and the tumultuous maelstrom closed in and around and that was it. Maybe? I don't know. Like others, I can only imagine.

What is it like? The exhibits consisted of people's spectacles, children's toys and household items misshapen by the intense heat. There are stories of great courage and evidence of the effects of radiation that impregnated grotesque malformations, thus babies were born that looked like hideous creations. A famous exhibit in the museum is a wristwatch set in time at eight fifteen in the morning, on 'the' morning and there it is. For many people, their life stopped at the time shown on the face of the watch but here life continues, in the museum where people are attempting to maintain an awareness of what happened. It is there as a warning for all of us. It's a symbol. I mean the whole of the Peace Memorial Park which has many memorials. There is the Flame of Peace which it is said will continue to burn until there is not one nuclear weapon remaining on this Earth that we all share. It's a nice sentiment but it's a big ask and I wouldn't think the money mongers will allow that to happen so the chances of the flame being extinguished are pretty remote. There is the Children's Peace Memorial where there are thousands of paper cranes, folded by school children in the memory of a young girl who had leukaemia, an effect of the radiation. The crane symbolises long life and happiness. The young girl attempted to fold a thousand paper cranes but didn't live to reach her target so the task was continued by other school children which spread throughout Japan. The cranes are taken or sent to the memorial in her memory. There are memoirs, photographs, personal belongings and accounts of what life was like just after the bomb exploded and there is a hall and places to contemplate and pray and give thoughts to those who lost their lives, to the survivors and to the ensuing suffering. Not all victims of the atomic bomb were Japanese; it is said that over one in ten or even one in seven of the victims were Korean. They were people forcibly taken from their country to work as slave labourers in Japanese factories. It just gets grimmer.

In the corridors and on the stairways of the museum, there is a steady press of people, young and old, reminding me of religion in that it felt like the converted congregation gathering at a Mecca. It was respectful and mournful, its message accepted with a quietude having no hint of dissent. The young school children rush along in a hail of clamour and yet to be bridled fun, holding their project folders, running and then slowing and hushing one another. The peace sign flicked with small fingers, standing for the photo pose. Many of them looking like Dee Dee Ramone when he was a young man.

I watched some films that were taken during those times just after the atomic bomb exploded about one minute's walk from where I was standing. There were films about the amount of nuclear bombs existing in the world and of how many times the world could be destroyed by the amount of bombs that have been produced. There were figures and statistics and information on environmental problems and warnings to the safety of our future and indeed the existence of the planet called Earth if big business and power hungry politicians are allowed to continue with their ways. It was all very virtuous in its intent. I looked around at other exhibits and I know it might seem out of place to say it but something felt missing. It was as if there was a gap, a piece not being there that made up the whole and it came to me at first with the thought that not everyone who suffered in the Second World War was Japanese because this is how I felt it was coming across to me. It was as if it was only the Japanese.

Although the environmental message of warning to the future of all life on our planet included everyone in all parts of the world, it asked for us all to be conscious of the effects we are having on what is called nature or the natural environment. I started to look around the museum for information about other people who were victims besides the Japanese. Maybe I had missed it but I didn't see anything about the Koreans and of how they were treated in such a brutal manner in having to live underground and used as slave labour for the Japanese and the intrusion that was made upon people living on the Islands in that part of the world and the Chinese and the others and of course the many Japanese themselves who suffered at the hands of Japans' military. There could and might well be evidence and information in other areas in the peace park but I couldn't find anything in the building that I was walking about in.

I watched the bodily movements and expressions of the people milling around the different exhibits whether it was a twisted artefact in a glass case or watching a film. Some of the people stood wearily as if being war worn themselves, shifting weight from one foot to the other, slowly shaking their heads, pressing lips together and looking down. I noticed an American couple, meaning they were from the USA. The woman wiped a tear that was ready to break and run down her cheek and the man stood still, solemn as if reflecting as he gazed at whatever it was he was looking at as if he was actually there when it happened or that it was his fault.

There might well have been people visiting the museum who had a connection to what happened on the 6th August 1945. An American visitor might well have had a relative who was in the air force or was a prisoner of war because there were some of those killed by the bomb. The Japanese people in the museum could well have been related to people who were involved in what happened; and the others and then I thought, 'and the others', but then 'we' are all involved. It doesn't matter at the end of the day who is telling their side of the story because we all have a story, because we are all involved. I didn't like the way my thinking was taking me, seeing the Japanese as being selective in their biased telling of the experience of war with all its horrors and suffering. Everyone does it and all of us have a vein of hypocrisy running through us. So I stopped my train of thought, of going down that route of tit for tat and I just allowed the essence and the experience of being in the museum to move slowly though me as I stood with others whoever they were and gawped at the grotesque that the human imagination has reified for our disconcertment.

We stood up and looked at an actual sized replica of Little Boy that was hung on the wall. It was much smaller than I had imagined it to be. To think that something being just that size could unleash such devastation. I imagined the people who put it together, the manual workers moulding the casing in a factory, checking the metal welding for flaws and then the boffins overseeing the insertion of the components into the casing being hopeful for its positive function and then maybe having thoughts to the fate of the human race and then, maybe, a man or a woman gave a final wipe with a cloth on the metal case that held the ticking bomb and placed the cloth in his or her pocket and thought about what tea or supper he or she will be having and then maybe the bomb was wheeled to a place in the factory where it was later picked up and taken to another place, maybe by a man who drove the truck and he was just going through the motions that made up his working day and all the while the bomb was nestling quiet and cosy in its safe metal sheaf, a tragic womb, created by man and the baby is a monster for when given birth, this Little Boy will make his presence felt. There will be no concerns of him being shy or over sensitive by anxious parents. No, mummy and daddy are scientists and they will stand outside the fence of the school playground, their folders and ledgers assiduously checked and added to in the dispassionate posturing that takes place in the process of objectification as they measure and judge their creation, the bouncing baby Little Boy as he makes his intrusion. And way over in Japan, in the back of a house in Hiroshima, a young girl plays with a new doll that an aunty gave her and the little girl places the doll with the others that she has, not fully happy with the name that she has given the new doll and she tucks them into their bed, all safe and she tells the dolls, as she points to each one in turn, pointing her chubby finger into the face of each doll, that if they behave themselves she will take them out the following morning and buy them a treat before she goes to school and maybe the following day is her birthday and that's why she is excited and she's feeling a little more older than she did the day before, like a real grown up and some of the dolls are being silly and acting like little children and she remembers what the date is tomorrow because it's her birthday, see - it's the 6th August and the year is 1945.

I shook the imagery from my mind, feeling choked at the dark scene I had evoked.

I took a final look at the replica of the bomb and turned away with my mind flitting around as flashing thoughts made comparisons between the two opposing actors in the theatre of war. I thought of how evasive and puke inducing it is to use such farcical language. Terminology that sounds inoffensive as it is recited by a sugary double act that is the norm now in presenting what is called the news. It's a him and her act, choreographed, the director always striving for different settings and where to place the presenters. Age, looks and sex appeal have transcended everything and seen as far more important than the material which the puppet-like presenters present. Their performance in these programmes or shows is entertainment and what the presenters look like and their relationship with each other and the style of engaging the consumer is a matter of most importance and it will lock facile people in meetings as they discuss the style and delivery of their product. It doesn't matter because the same news is read out on the different stations so the act is all in the fickle superficiality that is the mask that takes precedence over the subject matter.

The perversity of it all is easily apparent for all to see. Blessing inanimate objects is explained through a thing called religion in the East but that also exists in the West where there is also reverence given to objects. Objects like bombs for example, are revered for their power that can be used to maintain what we call freedom. I remember watching the news at a time when the UK was preparing itself for combat with another nation. An item was shown that also appeared in newspapers, where very young school children were engaged in a school project under the supervision of teachers to make their contribution to the war effort. The children were designing colourful creations in that childish way using only primary colours and then the creation was to be put on the side of bombs; bombs to be dropped on other children in another place but because they're different maybe it doesn't matter. The teacher praises the child and smiles at his or her near toothless grin for making a beautiful gesture, maybe a colourful depiction of a rainbow over a house and flames coming from another house that has been hit by a bomb, a house where they live; a bomb dropped by the brave man, like 'daddy the hero'.

I pondered over the uncomfortable thoughts that entered my mind. The tiredness that one feels when travelling began to feel like a weight bearing down upon me and just as I was about to chastise myself for being so pessimistic, I stopped myself from doing so. If I didn't have such thoughts, I wouldn't be a thinking person. If a place like the museum didn't trigger thoughts that question our behaviour and possibly our fate in a person's mind, then I would say that the person's mind is little more than an ice rink, being just an unthinking strip from which all matter simply skates off.

I read from a board a story that was written by a witness to the bomb and for some bizarre and indefensible reason, I grinned to myself. It may well have been a defence mechanism or a coping strategy to manage matters that are horrific and shocking. I don't know. Maybe it's just me being a sicko and it's mixed with the hard-edged irony that makes up a large part of the humour emanating from the culture that I have experienced. The story or the account that I was reading told of how survivors referred to the bomb as Pika (flash of light) Don (tremendous sound). I wondered if some punk band had ever been called this. 'Pika Don' and that maybe they had and were famous but I wouldn't know. I thought about some of the people that I have known and worked with in my life, some of the men who exhibit the archetypical geezer behaviour that certain builders have from the London area. I could easily envisage that the term Pika Don would be a euphemism for the morning after in the bathroom after a fiery Ruby Murry in sauce as hot as Hiroshima.

The place was grim. It was meant to be – I'm not that thick. It held evidence to the atrocity created by humans and there was no excuse this time of blaming it on the other or acting like animals. There was an acceptance of the human way to vent the perverse propensity for self- destruction. The museum gave urgent warnings regarding the use of nuclear power and the perils of the so-called arms race.

I walked outside and decided to make my way across the memorial park. Over a little bridge from where I was standing was the A-Bomb Dome. It's the famous building (or what remains of it) that has been left as it was after the bomb exploded directly above that area. It's left in its shattered state as a reminder for all to see and has now been snapped by God knows how many cameras as the 'must see' relic to the nightmarish event. As I walked down the steps of the museum a man on a pushbike stopped me. He asked me how I was and if I was an American. "Nothing to do with me," I said and smiled at him. I told him that I was English. We had a chat about world politics, American foreign policy and where it will all lead. He lied when he told me that we are lucky to live in a democracy and that America is making the world a place where people can be free. After half a minute of discussing the possible contradictions in some of his theory, he admitted that humans haven't evolved from 'might is right' and that we have to get on with it. This man told me that he was sixty seven years of age. He was about nine when the bomb went off. I asked him about it. What memory had he of it and where was he at the time. He told me that he lived in the countryside, sixty kilometres from Hiroshima. He heard no sound. The Don hadn't reached as far as his area but there was thick black smoke high in the air and drifting everywhere. His father went into town straight away because he had friends who had gone there for the markets and such like. He told me that his father was affected by the radiation and that it most probably killed him in the end.

I asked him how old his dad was when he died. "Eighty five," he told me. I took a long look at this character. Eighty five. That's the kind of age that neurotics and lunatics go on special diets for and join health clubs and take up exercise routines with hopes of living into their eighties. I felt like saying to him that his dad should have been given a medal or had a memorial stone erected in his honour for being the fittest survivor of the Second World War. We had a chat about life in general. He told me he cycles to be healthy and that he speaks English at any opportunity he can. He thanked me for my time.

We both went into the library that is in the park. He was going in there to do some research. I was going in there to use the toilet. The man didn't have a job but was desperate to do something useful with his time. We shook hands again, something I don't mind doing. I also like meeting people and when you take the outside track in life, you bump into the non-competitors, the wanting and those that are lonely in their place on the side of things. I thought it would have been nice if he could of had a job for a few hours a week talking to English speaking tourists, telling his tale. He could talk of rural life around Hiroshima during that time, the names of people that he knew, of how the Japanese civilians were treated by the State, the way that people lived, their diet and their feelings. Maybe even talk about foreign people like prisoners of war and the Korean people used as slave labour and of what he or other people thought about them. It would be his experience, subjective and meaningful. There would be no need for people to buy books that are written by people who weren't there. It would be nice if that small but very real picture was given, the one with honest truth about it, having the imperfections of people and their daily life, not the one that fits into fashionable acceptance. But then, for the most part, the world isn't a nice place.

I watched him carry his cycle clips up the stairs in the library and I looked through the window, across the park at the A-Bomb Dome. There is an imbalance in it all. I walked across the park and over the concrete bridge towards the A-Bomb Dome. I stood by the bridge and watched the ever-present crowds of school children huddled in groups striking poses from mimicking pop groups to the traditional school assembly fashion, the two finger peace sign in evidence, always. The girls with their sailor blues and the boys in that distinctive naval tunic. I looked at the peace signs that the school children held up and wondered how long it will be before it is replaced by the devil's forked hand gesture that is shown in western photo calls from Rap bands. I thought of that gesture meaning the peace sign. It looked mechanical but then that isn't just a Japanese trait, the same is evident in all cultures.

The Dome itself is fenced off. I watched people taking photographs of it, the school children and adults, smiling, with the debris of radioactive bricks and metal as a backdrop to a day trip that had been dutifully performed and can now be ticked from the list of necessary activities. I didn't take any photographs in Hiroshima. It wasn't a conscious decision not to. I just didn't. I didn't think of it, what with looking around and thinking about what had happened and all the ensuing contradictions. My mind wasn't fixed on doing the expected thing to do, to take home a snap shot of the notorious place with the ominous history. Yet, of course, Hiroshima wasn't the only Japanese city to get a morning call from Uncle Sam's flying delivery service of hate. Three days later on the 9th August, there was another morning drop at about 10:48am in the city of Nagasaki. The name of the plane was Bock's Car. It carried an atomic bomb much more powerful than the one dropped on Hiroshima. The name given to this bomb was 'Fat Man'. Little Boy goes to Hiroshima and the Fat Man goes to Nagasaki. The American military showing their subtle wit although I don't know if it could ever be accommodated in a thing called humour. The atomic bomb exploded directly above a Catholic church in Nagasaki and then life became a chaotic place of the damned and as in the case of Hiroshima, amongst the multitude of tens of thousands of people who died, there was an estimated thirteen thousand Korean slave labourers who had their lives extinguished in a land that they had been forced to be in.

I turned and walked away from the twisted heap of bygone building materials and rested on a seat, looking around myself, wondering if the air was still contaminated. The park had a leisurely atmosphere that was intended for rumination and education, having a mission to inform, to remind people to remember and to act as a warning. I felt the whole thing was on the verge of becoming passé. The Japanese want to survive and be successful in a present world where there is the rush to compete. Remembrance has its place but not as a preponderance and some see it serving as a function to exploit. Maybe the writing is already on the wall. For some there is a declining interest in what happened. There have been acts of vandalism in the Memorial Park by Japanese people wanting to raise awareness to present problems like unemployment and the long hours people have to work when they get a job and the insecurity of it all. People who are of an age who lived through the war are dying and the Prime Minister had recently stopped performing a previous duty to meet them. There is a strong lobby from those representing the nuclear industry, warning of problems if Japan doesn't use nuclear power. In the evolving nature of change, the future generations will utilise whatever they can to adapt in order to survive.

An Australian girl asked me the way to the museum in a manner that suggested that I didn't speak English. I gave her my map. A couple of hours was all that I wanted around there. I walked to the tram stop. Having plenty of time before the bullet train took me to Kyoto, I strolled through the park in the direction of the road that runs outside of it. As I stepped onto the tram I heard American accents, one of them came from a man in his late forties. He was with his wife and child and his mother-in-law who was Japanese but had lived in the United States of America for a long time. It felt as though I hadn't had a proper conversation with someone for ages. I mean in a lucid way because of the language thing. I had given directions to the girl from Australia a few minutes earlier but as I said, it felt a lifetime since I had a proper chat which told me how much I like to speak to people. I was beginning to feel numb. Making yourself understood for the most simplistic acts of communication caused a reticence in asking a question as I knew it would become convoluted and I would end up making slapstick humour to diffuse embarrassment as is my way for I am so insecure and lacking in confidence; but, enough already. Yet, I learned a thing about myself and that is I need to be or maybe I'm just used to, talking with people all the time. How does it feel for those people who travel alone in the most remote areas having only their own company and the relationship they build with nature? I had always considered myself as a person who understood the feeling of being separate from the mainstream and to live a solitary existence but a day with no one to bleat at in a way that I feel comfortable with and I'm going stir-crazy or something like that.

On hearing the man's accent, I spoke to him. I asked a vacuous question that I knew the answer to but it was an excuse just to speak to someone. I said, "Do we pay when we get off or are we meant to pay now?" He looked at me. It was a cross between being confused and shock. Leaning his head close to me he said, "I beg your pardon?" Again I asked the stupid question and then again because he didn't answer but just looked at me. The feeling of a heavy weight came upon me and I thought, "Oh no, maybe this is how it will be for the rest of my life," even though I imagined he or other people spoke in a language I thought I understood to be my own, they would not be able to understand me. I felt the bars slam across my chest, trapped in a private world, one where everything was decided by me because I didn't or couldn't relate to anyone else and it wasn't anything to do with the language thing because it was my mind that had slipped, making my needs incomprehensible for 'normal' people to comprehend. It would be a condition that consigned me to a place where I was outside of all activities that are deemed commonplace with people all over the world.

So I asked again and I felt myself being a little impatient but again the bloke didn't seem to understand what I was saying. I changed the way of asking the extremely simple question to something like, "Do you know by what means we have to pay on this tram?" But he just stared at me. So I tried again. "Is it the custom to pay when getting off?" It was hopeless. I asked him if he spoke English. "Sure," he said, looking at me closely in a way a psychologist might look at a prospective patient who could offer a lucrative amount of cash in research grants. It was as if I could hear the ice crack. Normal transmission had resumed. He suddenly understood what I was saying and I nearly said something like, "That was weird," referring to the language barrier problem we seemingly had for twenty odd seconds but I then decided it might confuse things again. We cleared up the matter of paying and if you are interested, we had to pay when we left the tram.

He told me that he had been to England. He then pointed out the members of his family standing next to him on the bus and I told him of my visits to his country. Our hurried conversation slid into matters of culture and I brought up writing, telling him John Steinbeck was a big favourite of mine. He called his wife over. She told me that John Steinbeck's sister was at their wedding and her name was Beth Ainsworth. She was an old lady at the time of their wedding but unfortunately had since died. The man's wife asked me why I liked John Steinbeck. I told her my reasons, mainly that the subjective experiences of so called ordinary people are principal in exposing or looking at the reasons why people are in the positions that they are. I spoke to her of class and she spoke to me of class but in that way that I have often heard Americans talk, having a conception of class that is different, seeing problems of poverty, unemployment and child mortality as somehow existing separately from the State. There are myths of well paid manual workers where 'those guys are doing alright' but the question of healthcare and all the rest is often negated in this reasoning. She told me that the same people, in type and family, still run the town where John Steinbeck came from. The people who discarded him, seeing him as a trouble making socialist and the like. A few years ago, the town's fathers said they would build a monument or something to show that one of America's greatest writers came from there. But John Steinbeck's son or sons told them to stick it and if they want to erect something then build a tenpin bowling alley in his remembrance as they thought this is what John Steinbeck would have considered to be in keeping with their way.

The tram reached Hiroshima station. The American man and his family went off to check the 'luggage 'an all'. I sat outside a small shop that was a bakery but within twenty seconds I had succumbed and went in to buy various pastries. I came back out and sat on a cycle stand to feed my overfed face whilst watching the coming and going into the station.

It struck me again how many school children there were. Nowhere seemed complete without their presence. In a way there seemed to be an over abundance of them, legions of them, some in uniformed lines on organised school outings or just trailing along in mass groups or straggling pairs, usually giggling and laughing in a state of high excitement at the prospect of extreme competition for employment in later life and the bonus of having to do a sixteen hour day when they found jobs. But, the Japanese do make a nice apple and icing pastry or bun or whatever they are called. I found a more comfortable spot to sit. Having plenty of time until my train left, I sat there and watched but what was I watching? It came to me. I was looking for deformed people. A middle-aged man wearing a suit came along on crutches. I watched as he heaved himself along. He was a man in miniature having shrunken legs that were useless, for standing and walking that is. He held a brief case in one hand as he pushed down on to his crutches that were buried deep into the sockets of his narrow shoulders. I realised that this was what I was idly looking for. Disfigured people. The people that were deformed as a result of the atomic bomb that crushed and melted our fellow humans and animal comrades and then the air was sullied with hideous poison that was breathed in and the food and water was polluted. Consequently, the desired effect was established of causing mass cruelty and suffering for years to come.

Why shouldn't the school children be perpetually happy I thought to myself? But then I snapped myself out of that way of thinking. I'm just not optimistic enough to believe that some of these grinning school kids wouldn't love to get their grimy mitts on a power weapon and given the right breeding and turn of history, they might have and might do – who knows? I for one haven't a clue. Yet, I felt that beneath the self effacing smile beats a yearning for kamikaze action, the mask of relinquishment is in place and there is a showing of deference to others but for many there is a deep disliking for sloppy Joe's

An Unlikely Fooligan

Americana and a detestation of subservience. There are memories of a strong Japan that earned respect from others and even struck fear and there are the thoughts of Mishima. Of course not for all but all the same it does reside in the Japanese psyche. And as I sat there next to a cycle rack cursing myself for finishing all the apple buns topped with icing, I considered that there has already been a change in the modern Japan that was established after the Second World War because memories are weakening concerning the war and all that the country went through and suffered. The new approach can be seen to be developing a different philosophy in the strategy to survive. The economic success that was reached in the late 1980's has lessened. Japan is now looking at itself again. There is a process of re-evaluation. It wants greater autonomy and to build up military services. The business world has put pressure on government to change preceding policy in order to allow the businesses to have more power in dictating their terms without being constrained by government legislation that demands a responsibility for those that they employ. Terms and conditions have changed as the relationship between employer, the State and the employee has altered. Also deteriorating is the loyalty factor that has been seen as a traditional Japanese practice because unemployment has made a return and the responsibility will lie with the employee as the new attitude will be to paddle his/her own canoe. And with it will come all the other aspects and consequences of adopting the individualistic ideology that gives virtual carte blanche to big business to do as they wish. Things have changed in this part of the world for the Japanese, what with South Korea and North Korea and of course the old enemy China has attained for itself the status as being a leading world power and the Western States are ingratiating as they scurry around the potent giant.

I stopped my thoughts. It was a sunny day and I was on holiday but the feeling stayed with me. It's something that I can't shrug off because I am a watcher and I always take my metaphorical hand torch with me, shining it at what I see and find, trying to gain a clearer look and thus understanding. There is the other Japan residing besides that which is presented to a modern world. It exists in the importance of ritual as displayed and perpetuated by what might be seen as disparate individuals and groups participating in festivals and ceremonies that are sometimes understood as being religious. That doesn't matter because all action is significant to the here and now and is also relevant to spiritual beliefs. It isn't how it is often understood in the West as being a dualism. No, because it's a wholeness. It's played out and presented, celebrated and then internalised by the society en mass, then absorbed and integrated to strengthen the collective.

A young woman, she was about seventeen years of age I would guess, broke my thoughts as she clattered her motor scooter into one of the stands in the bike rack next to where I was sitting. I watched her as she fiddled and fastened the lock around the frame of her bike and the stand; in a country where people do not steal. She wore a retrospective heterogeneous mix and match outfit. I imagined it to be designer store clothing that is marketed at the student who aspired to be bracketed in the individualistic casual but chic range. She turned, running the fingers of one hand through her hair and carrying her crash helmet in the other and she skipped off.

I looked around at nothing in particular but at everything and the feeling that I had earlier on before going into the Memorial Park came back to me. The feeling of detachment, of separateness and I felt a sense of distance as if it had clunked into place but I was happy in being apart. I resided and relaxed with the feeling, contemplating the things that I had seen and the thoughts that I had during my two visits to Japan. My original thoughts of taking a holiday were just to have a break in a different culture although it turned out to be an examination of Japan. I thought about the different features and practices that when conjoined create Japan.

During my first visit my friend took me to a Sumo tournament in Tokyo. Sumo has its origins going back a couple of thousand years, being part of a ritual that hoped to gain favour in getting a good harvest. The procedures and ceremony retain Shinto beliefs although it has developed into a sport having a specific dress code, rules and regulations. Sumo is distinctively Japanese. It is a sport and a tradition. I was told that it is the only traditional sport that gets peak time television coverage. The wrestlers are nationally known figures and are highly esteemed heroes. The tournament is called a basho. The stadium that I went to was large and the crowd was a mixture of people who were young, old and in the middle. Men, women, boys and girls were there and it had a buzz. The guys are big and spend an age going through the preliminaries to the fight, doing the salt throwing and walking around in their ponderous way but they generate energy that charges up the crowd. As one might expect, the atmosphere in and around the stadium is civil. It's a well mannered affair having a communal feel. There are stalls selling food, souvenirs and a range of things in a market type ambience that encouraged people to browse and enjoy the event. In the actual arena, the seating is graded by the price one pays for the ticket. It is very corporate close to the raised ring where people are seated in small groups in boxes and chow down to a spread of food and booze. The seats we had were up and away but that being said exceptional value for one's yen when one considers the price of a ticket in Blighty to attend one of the national sports. I'd say the ticket price was a tenth or even a twelfth of what it costs to see a football, cricket or rugby match of the same type of quality of seating. Anyway, I didn't and don't know anything about Sumo and I'm not going to give you an outlined account here that I've skimmed from a tourist book or the like. Interestingly or surprisingly for me at any rate, there are champions in this sport that aren't Japanese. They are Mongolian and Hawaiian for example and are greatly revered despite being a foreigner. The wrestlers are called rikishi. I watched them walking around the stadium, dressed in their kimonos and sandals with their hair pulled back and bunched into a bun, usually in pairs, never alone, some with a ring of young people standing in front of them offering bits of paper or a programme to be autographed with cameras raised ready to click. They appeared arrogant as they ambled in a tired manner, conscious of their great size and presence and the attention that they get. When standing close to one of these men one realises the size of them and can sense the physical power that they possess. I noted that some of them walked with a smaller man by their side who was also dressed in a sumo costume. I thought that these men were a sort of an accomplice, an assistant of some kind. I didn't know but that's what I took them to be.

I thought about the respect that the sumo wrestler receives and of how the Japanese are proud of these big men and the contribution they make to the national identity. As I sat next to that bike rack, I smiled to myself for two reasons. One was the irony of having massive men as significant cultural heroes when one considers all the body fascists that exist in the West where bigness and being fat incites the most spiteful ridicule. It is seen as repulsive and blame is heaped upon the overweight people for being irresponsible and disregarding personal health matters and that they should be taxed at a greater rate because of their larger size. The second reason was the name rikishi. Rikishi becomes, with a bit of word play from a west London funster, Riki Shi. Riki Shi the wrestler. Riki Shi. He is no fooligan and he's Japan's top geezer. I had the amusing thought of keeping an eye out for the Japanese equivalent of the herbert geezer type that is found where I come from whilst on my saunter in TLOTRS and Riki Shi could be him. Was the geezer to be found in the guise of a Sumo wrestler? No, not at all is the quick answer to my light hearted question and association. He's an institution but then again, the behaviour and personality of the herbert geezer or Mr Herbert Geezer, is an established character in British culture, hanging around pubs in housing estates, driving his motor with his arm dangling out the window, sovereign rings bunched on his fingers that double up as legal knuckledusters and all the other examples of body language that are employed by Mr Herbert Geezer. What if Riki Shi existed in the land where I came from? It would be different now wouldn't it? 'Riki Shi is a fat-un'. I can see it sprayed on the shutters of a shop in an estate somewhere in England or scrawled on the door in the toilets of a pub – 'Riki Shi is a fat queer'. In the TLOTRS nobody giggles whilst in a school playground somewhere in West London, a young herbert would spray on a wall, 'Riki Shi can't get his end away' and other such demeaning remarks because in TLOTRS the big rucking lumps have been accommodated and given credence. Their behaviour, character and presentation has been afforded a space within the system and has become an orthodox constitution itself. For just a second, let's forget the historical rationalization and the pontificating concerning the origins and importance of Sumo and culture because anything can be talked up if there is the will to do so and for whatever purposes that might be. Let's be honest and I don't mean to be base but those screaming little girls, excited old ladies and indeed excited men who gaze at Riki the grunter and his lumpen mates haven't the tradition of an ancient ritualised performance with its origins in the Shinto belief system on their febrile minds. No, no they have not.

The big fat bloke is respected in Japan and I reflected upon this. I thought about the people who occupy positions of authority back home who dictate what is appropriate and what isn't and they seemed so dry and insipid. My mind returned to the big men of battle who will nod a respectful and humble bow to the cheque given to them from one of the giant companies that is seen as God in this isle. Here the massive man takes his reward for he is an esteemed elite warrior accepting his worth, a token showing benevolence and power from the massive company that perpetuates the system, for it has replaced and maybe they are little different from, the powerful ancestral overlords giving privilege to its nobles and mighty combatants and the massive man who has no physical equal amongst his human peers is just a grateful child servant and nods obediently to his master. The short life expectation and assiduous training will prosper only but a handful of these mammoth chumps to be champs dressed in their baby nappy range of weirdo paedo paraphernalia but these aren't lumps for lampooning. No, their arduous physical programme does make them regarded as the most proficient martial artist and who's going to ague with them? Their phlegmatic lumbering stroll of a walk is an antithesis to the common Japanese walking manner. Whilst one will often see women doing a little dainty run to speed them along as they perform their duties, men on the other hand, manoeuvre themselves in quick footed twists and nod an apology for getting in one's way. The general pace can be frenetic but then what's this colossal being casting its significant shadow on the embers of the rising sun? It's Riki Shi - blundering along, wiping tears from his eyes as he grieves the demise of the light that once shone from that sun.

'Embers?' Did I say 'embers?' I did indeed. For I foresee the end to the entity known as The Land of the Rising Sun - I think. Yes - yes I do, oh reader of this account that is put together by a warped Western clocking machine - which is my good self - being ignorant to most things, naive but belligerent, frequently wrong but believing my honest character will excuse my clumsy mishandling of nearly everything I get close enough to hold on to - but I'm usually wrong - of course I am - it's only my opinion anyway - the gaze and listless thought of a marginal man.

And here in TLOTRS, I walk about alone, living out my role as one of God's lonely men and what do I do? Instead of trying my luck at trying to hitch up with some graceful little lady and feel the closeness of her soft nubile body beneath her silken kimono, I wander with thoughts of my childhood when then I also walked a random stroll and watched all that was about me. At the age of eight, I walked around the wide roads within the confines of an American air base that was close to where I lived. My khaki shorts not fitting properly, a worn snake belt buckled tightly in an attempt to hold the folds of khaki cloth up my skinny waist and I looked down at my worn sandals and the grey socks that I wore to school but this was the summer holidays and it was sunny and warm and I was in a different land. I was in the land of the American soldier and I looked up at the big men in their uniforms. I saw them as kind and good men. Men who I would be safe in asking directions to, yet nervous of course for I was just a boy but feeling secure by these good men. I asked questions that didn't need to be asked. Asking where the entrance to the base was when I knew very well where it was; or if they had the time when I had no need of knowing what time it was anyway; or if I was walking in the right direction to reach the amusements that had been put on for the 4th July celebrations when it was obvious where they were because one could see the constructions of fun from where I was and hear the music and smell that smell that I understood as being American which was the smell of fat and sugar. An excitement purred in my stomach at the opulence of it all and the informality and the slack and easy attitude. It was different, yet being in an area close to where I lived, just a fenced off bit of land but the smells and sights, the cars, the clothing people wore and the way the children dressed was from the land that I saw on the television which was a vague place of images being alien to me. But here it was, in the air base near to where I lived. I would see children on a large yellow bus with the steering wheel on the other side from what I was used to and I had seen the children before outside the confines of the base, sitting on the bus holding bags and dressed in clothes that were not available in the shops at that time when there were no large stores. The children didn't wear school uniforms. They slumped lazily in their seats wearing jeans, most having colourless faces, a result I was told from having central heating in their homes – another myth constructed to discredit the other and thus create a sense of superiority of one's own culture. But the children were different in that they responded in a lethargic manner when spoken to by an adult, having torpid gazes and movements and a whining slurred speech. Yes, I watched as the children were bussed from one area to another, these being the children of men and women who were in the services serving the United States of America. Whilst walking inside the base, I would think of the land that I had seen images of on the television, a land of My Favourite Martian, Run Buddy Run, Hawaii Five O, Seventy Seven Sunset Strip – grown men wearing the clothes grown men didn't wear, like slacks and jeans, Tee shirts and shirts that had bold checks and loud prints, sunglasses and there were fat ladies wearing bright green stretched trousers called pants and the motion of jaws moving silently as they chewed gum and I felt it all unlike but familiar because of the television. I felt my poverty, the smallness of everything about me and the cheapness in quality. I mean none of the American children were dressed like me. I was like something out of a black and white film depicting refugee children from the Second World War. Any tiny material item was seized upon like people would who are trapped on a desert island. I noticed the easy nonchalance of the American kid as he threw away half of a candy bar and scuffed the sole of his sneaker without concern. I saw them all as wealthy but I was wrong. Of course I was. And the men looked different. Some were Chinese looking but had the American accent and the men in uniform were real, having come to life now that I was inside the base and many of them were tall, very tall with unbelievably shiny caps on their boots. They were always kind. They were more relaxed and informal than the adults I was used to interacting with. "Yes sir," some of them would say. "Now you have yourself a nice day," I was told by men wearing uniforms. It was very different from what I would have expected if I had spoken to a man in an army uniform coming from the country that I was brought up in. And the jeeps and other motor vehicles were larger and better. It seemed as if they weren't real and then it felt as if nothing was real. It was a hazy bliss where things were different. There was no strangled feeling of reprimand. This was a place of abundance, of candy, of hot dogs and burgers. I would continue in asking questions of the big men in uniform just to make contact for I was alone. "Get yourself a soda and something to eat, now," I was told and I nodded politely and said, "Thank you."

Now here in TLOTRS, the same child only years older and now called an adult and because of that perceived as being different but none of us change, I believe, only some of us more than others hang on to emotions that were felt as a child. Here in Japan, my gaze is the same and that thing, that feeling that I had during my first trip to this country a year earlier had now fallen into place as I understood what it was that it reminded me of and it niggled me for the want of needing to be resolved. It was the American airbase back home – that is what is was – and I realised that I was like Master Samurai who hadn't shaken off images from his childhood, images that he has added value and emotions to, built out of proportion, being unreal, in fact delusional. But then that's not his fault because the conditioning is created to cheat and deceive, so it isn't our fault, so there! Revolving in his mind is a time when he will be taking a scotch on the rocks in a darkened bar and nibbling the cherry from the glass that is held by the girl who is a platinum blond and is falling from her stall right into his lap. Yes, Master Samurai, there he is and sitting the other side of him is a character from the pen of Raymond Chandler, all square jawed, brazen as a bullet, carrying an injury from the war but now dressed slicker than an Italian's haircut as he goes about his business that is shadier than a closed down cinema, his blue jaw moving over a piece of gum and he shoots Master Samurai a look that shows that the colour of his eyes are blue and lonely and this ex GI shrugs his great muscular shoulders and picks up his iced glass from the bar. He raises it; who to? Well, Master Samurai, of course and so it was with me, the representation of the USA that I saw as a child. The image of easy affluence is a seductive tablet and I swallowed mine because I was guileless and I still am, of course.

* * * * * * * *

I stopped thinking or I tried to and I stood up and stretched my magnificent torso, the body that is the number one fantasy for a million Japanese schoolgirls, having a picture of me in a little heart shaped trinket hanging from their mobile phones, the previous one which was David Beckham has been removed, screwed up and thrown away. I laughed but not out loudly at the thought of this and then pondered a little disconcertingly why I had thought it. But, enough already. I slung the strap of my bag over my shoulder, drew out the handle on the suitcase and pulled it into the station.

I went and spoke to a man in the ticket booth about the train I intended to catch, things like what platform or track it was leaving from and at what time. The railway workers are extremely helpful, every one of them. They were never anything but helpful and professional as I approached them carrying my railway pass or a map and a ticket and always with a dazed look on my face. They must have seen it a few thousand times before at the busy stations that is. A figure looming towards them, slowly pointing with an absent expression to a map or phrase book. That grin that comes from feeling awkward but I never saw their eyes drop or raise or turn away or snap the pencil they might be holding or kick the side of their booth. No, they looked directly at the wandering foreigner, the outsider. They had a steady look that locked into me as he or she extended a hand to look at my map or book and his or her head would turn slightly to the side in order for my nebulous language to be heard above all other sounds around us. And in a way I thought of them to be the champions of Japan. That's what these men and women are. They are overseers as if watching the masses go about their activities. They are in control, maintaining order in a precise manner that never wavers from the rules. They are respected for the most part and I saw them as embodying an essence that reaches further and beyond that what one would normally understand to be the remit of a transport worker. They symbolise a spirit that has been torn from Japanese hands. They are maybe the last bastions, a lost link in a culture where this type of uniformed discipline is missing from the consciousness. The military has been subdued, the spirit of Japan has been dissipated by outsider intrusion but the railway staff deal unhindered with matters of importance to Japan's interests, maintaining and running an essential part of the infrastructure. It's a complex operation getting all those worker ants to their workplace on time and it's served and directed with an exactitude that pleases in a very Japanese way as railway staff wield their control over the complex grid that buzzes with human vibration that has a will of its own. It is here that the manifestation of the Japanese spirit still shows itself.

It isn't possible on a bullet train but on the local trains, one can sit behind the driver and look over his shoulder at the track that is to be traversed. That's me, the anorak, the middle-aged man travelling alone, wanting to sit behind the driver. My competition for such an activity are young boys aged from two years to about eleven. After that age, most drift into adolescence seeking pleasures to satisfy desires and needs that will confront, confuse and frustrate them for the rest of their lives. For it is only or is seen as should only be within the domain of the child's imagination that an excitement can be incited by sitting behind a train driver, the man, doing an impossibly adult thing and the child can only wonder at the spectacular feeling it creates and maybe have aspirations of fulfilling dreams of one day becoming a train driver or take on a role that is adult. For there, in front of them is the man, in control, having responsibility for others and knowledge of driving this great successful experiment that is called a train. And there were a couple of mothers that gave me a sideways or even long looks as I occupied the seat that maybe they had promised their son to have if he behaved himself earlier on in the day.

The train drivers are always immaculate in dress and presentation. Taking off their jackets as they take their seat in the cab of the train, a crisp white shirt and tie with the sleeves rolled up a few folds and always wearing white cotton gloves. As the train stands motionless in a station, the driver checks the instruments on the panel in front of himself and when the signal changes colour and the conductor rings the bell, the driver will point forward, pointing ahead, in a spiritual oneness, setting off, being part of this great esteemed creation, the train, man and machine together. A unison. Made from materials, this manifestation of human conception that is shaped and given personal names. It embodies emotions and realises the dream of man, an existential being, a reified extension of ourselves because our endeavours are made possible through invention. It is the synthesis of the physical and mental that makes it achievable, making things that we are not physically capable of doing to become an everyday occurrence and thus a common activity that is relied upon for the positive functioning of society. The machine with man is the way. It is the way and as the driver points forward, he and machine are one and we are one as we ride upon the machine. We move with the way, rolling along a track of steel rails leading from a railway station that will take us to another station for whatever reason that may be.

The staff do indeed look smart and orderly, dressed in their clean uniforms with their shiny peaked hats and white gloves. People are reprimanded for not standing in the allotted places that are marked on the platform. I was snapped at on more than one occasion by elderly staff for loafing where I shouldn't have been when a train was approaching the station, once by an old woman who scolded me, giving me commands and orders with a tongue so sharp they could have been delivered with a scythe. She sneered contempt at my bovine incompetence and this was watched by grown men in their business suits, looking at me but not catching my eye for they were just relieved that it wasn't one of them that had been in the wrong. They checked their feet as they stood dutifully between the painted lines.

There is the feeling of pride for having created the skilful organisation, engineering, policy planning and all that it entails to run a proficient and efficient railway system that is modern and envied by other countries. I felt there to be a respect for the system itself and for things that are civic and there was also something spiritual. And how would it have been if the McDonald Rockers back in 1945 hadn't diffused the Nippon party that had been growing with pride?

* * * * * * * * *

I found out what time my train was leaving and from what platform. There was still some time so I bought a cup of coffee and what I thought was a cake but on biting into it, expecting a sweet taste, I found that in fact it tasted of fish. I thought about how fish and seaweed finds itself everywhere in this country – fish and school children. I had time for a quick visit to the gents before the train departed. As I was on my way to the toilets, I walked past a stream of shops and cafes. I then saw something in a little cafe that made me stop. I didn't stand there and gawp at the scene that had caught my attention. No, I positioned myself to the side of the cafe, finding a space that gave me a good view of what I wanted to observe without being too obvious about it. I placed my bag on the ground and whilst pretending to be looking for something in one of its side pockets, I raised my head to partake in my favourite past time which is gazing upon life's activities from the side lines. What took my eye was being acted out on stools against the counter. She sat there in her sailor outfit, that peculiar school uniform. I would guess she was about fourteen years of age and looked bored. She had an air about her that was more distant than any land that could be found by travelling across the seas and like a sailor, she too was passing by. Her port was the arm of a man who looked about forty seven years of age and was dressed in the customary business suit. His eyes greased away from her glance when she looked up and his gaze settled on the cuff of her school blazer and then to her knee that was raised on the rest of a vacant stool next to her. She looked across the cafe at the signs that were written in English except they made no sense because they are just slogans out of context as if the language was enough just by being itself. An everyday saying was plastered in primary colours over a plastic wrapping of an edible consumable and I felt that if it were not edible, it wouldn't have made any difference. And I imagined that she thought, 'it makes no sense'. Maybe she had an English lesson at school that afternoon and she was picking up the language pretty good. She was thinking that she might go to the United States of America, work in the media, fashion, journalism that was connected with the media and fashion - anyhow, yeah - 'the States' - have an apartment, drive a cool car - maybe have her own office with her name written on the door - she would bring her family and close friend over, pay for them as she would have enough money to treat them, well not all her family - her family except her brother, she wouldn't want him coming over - so that left just mum and dad - her brother can stay at home and look after the dog, that's if he's still alive by then - the dog that is. The waxen skinned man in the dark suit looked from the girl to the cash register. It was time to leave. "Here we go," maybe this is what she thought. But then maybe she wasn't nervous, this might have been her third, fourth or fifth time, each time with a different man in order to get the money to buy the much craved for designer goods that the young women and girls parade to other girls and young women. It made sense but then it made no sense.

And I thought about what I had just thought, 'sense'. What kind of word or meaning is that to ascribe to such a situation? This is a major railway station and this liaison between a man, a forty seven year old man and a fourteen year old girl is happening in everyday life as if it is a traditional practice, a consensual act between two people and the passing people comply to this custom. Foreigners accept it as being a cultural norm, even the ones that I have spoken to who pretend to hold enlightened values but here it is accepted with a fake worldly shrug of the shoulders and passed further away with a bitter grin. This is during the day in a public place for Christ's sake in a country known for its politeness and in a society whereby women are expected to present feminine graciousness. Call me naïve. She is only a girl. He is a grown man and all she wants is a hand bag. It is poverty in the way that the meaning of the word can bring together the two words deprived and depraved. I walked towards the platform where my train would be leaving from, the words 'masks' and 'concealment' kept coming to mind the more I looked about myself.

Eight

As I sat on the train that was on its way to Kyoto where I planned to stay for a couple of nights, I began to wonder about how difficult it was going to be to get a room. The language difficulty really was a problem and at times when pointing to the phrase or term in my book, it still didn't make sense to the mystified inhabitant who often, although being caring and had made an effort, would step back and shake his or her head, admitting defeat by being stumped by the bulky foreigner's question. The smooth running on the continuous rail track had the effect that meditation has by relaxing the mind and the body to a point where one has to force oneself not to drop off into sleep. It is in that space between sleep and being awake, that grey area of consciousness that holds onto thoughts and ideas where perceptions are realised differently from the norm when we are strung out by keeping pace with the demands of everyday life. This isn't a rare state to be in for a person like myself where daydreaming is very much the normal state of being, in fact it is quite typical. My thoughts flitted over the images and sounds of the day, all bedded on an insecurity of where I would be staying that night. The tone of voice and gesticulations of the Japanese people grew in my mind to an extent of being bizarrely grotesque. The delirious echoes of the day and preceding days ran though the drifting thoughts that spun around and from within my heated brain. I thought of the Japanese people and how the individual is presented and of how the society in which they live has provided a structure to accommodate acceptable presentations of self. I thought of the fooligan image, of his supposed personality and character – he is portrayed as the British geezer. I reflected on that part of British culture and on the ways that he, the geezer, openly displays through his physical social manners the innate psychological quandary that is within. The presentation has a learned conduct and incorporated within it are the signals and symbols that testify and demarcate the actor as he presents his self within whatever social situation he is involved. There is the declaration of being masculine and gratefully ignorant of 'silly girly' objects to a point of celebrating an instinct from the cave and the multi-layered discourse with all its vague and contradictory complexities that exist in the orthodox world of modernity. From an early age, the young actor who aspires to a geezer presentation of self learns to emulate tone and accent of voice, body language and the cultural referencing that will equip the young actor to successfully perform the role of being a geezer.

And I thought of the discrediting notions that exist about the Japanese. They have been stigmatised by the events of the Second World War and successfully so in being seen as having blind allegiance to authority and 'other' in comparison to the free expressing individualism that we enjoy in the West. And as the bullet train zipped along smooth rails that forged tracks through flat Japanese country, I pondered the processes of social conditioning, of its use and of how those processes are at work in everyday society to shape, bracket and label people for purposes of consumerism and State control. Holiday thoughts! A fish tasting like an apple doughnut becomes the smiling face of a fourteen year old school girl, the burning flesh of a young child becomes the freakishly deformed body of a new born infant and an insurmountable shower of babbling voices in a tone and language that is foreign to me began to come together – and then I was conscious of a person sitting near to me who wasn't there before. Before when? Before I had slipped into a near fevered sleep and I tried to wrestle from my mind an image of a geezer in a west London pub, shouting out his feelings, pushing the point home with his hand that holds a glass of beer, his little finger raised, every finger having a gold chunky ring and then he turns and speaks surreptitiously into the ear of a man who nods – and the young girl pushes the trolley down the aisle of the carriage in the bullet train that is whooshing through flat fields and passing the Japanese equivalent of L.S. Lowry's matchstick men – people going about their lives, as if disparate but all involved together – and then I look again at the red dot at the end of the carriage that charts the progress of our journey and I see that it has moved along a considerable distance in what seemed no time at all.

* * * * * * * * *

The tubby foreigner alighted from the bullet train at Kyoto station in early evening. He pulled a blue suitcase and had a bag over his shoulder. In one of his hands, he held a piece of paper. Written on it was the name of a hotel, the street that it was on and the nearest subway station to the hotel. It was written down three times, once in Japanese, once in a kind of pigeon Japanese and again in English. The station was busy and far too convoluted for the man on the ticket barrier to be able to give the directions that I needed. I went into one of the shops in the concourse at the station's entrance and after much befuddlement and with the help of a few people, I walked to a subway station and caught a train that took me a couple of stops. I exited the train and repeated the performance of asking people if they could help me, only this time it was just the street and the hotel that needed to be found. One of the men who helped me went through an elaborate mime in explaining where the hotel was and again, I hoped that I nodded and smiled at the appropriate time as he drew shapes in the air, widened his eyes and laughed at seemingly nothing. Then on pointing in the direction that I should be heading, I was pulled back after only taking a few steps as an afterthought was added by the good Samaritan to aid me further. Yet, I did find the hotel. Although nothing was written in English, only hieroglyphics that with tiredness enhanced the surreal nature of everything and a dead wall blocked all comprehension in a way that made me wonder for no longer than a second that maybe this was the total composition that is the nature of human endeavour and it is the way it will always be for the human kind, until it all stops as we know it. I went into the foyer of the hotel and recited from the piece of paper from the pigeon Japanese section, a pronunciation for the name of the hotel. It was met with an expression of bafflement on the young lady's face as she was stopped her in her tracks. She stood behind the reception desk, her expression was a cross between the anxiousness displayed when playing for time if you were being held up in some kind of robbery and are waiting and praying for help to come and a frozen look that penetrated me with a question, "Is everybody as mad and as different as you are where you come from?" Things did settle themselves and another member of staff, a young man, joined us for the great debate that developed into a situation that I felt symbolised in a microcosm the misunderstanding and ignorance that retards human interaction. I booked into a single room for two nights. The young man who had joined us laughed and he walked backwards, continuing to laugh now that the matter had been dealt with. I liked him. Who wouldn't?

The language was really a problem though, wanting to find out something simple like if one has to hand one's key in when leaving the hotel would turn into a circus of grinning and bowing and I would play my part in the fiasco by going through my slapstick routine of miming in great caricature movements what I was attempting to convey. This would make the girl laugh and she would nod her head and just when I thought that she understood and that it was all sorted out, she would then pull on an expression of bewilderment, frown and we would start again. "Towels and keys," I cursed to myself. Such an easy thing to organise and on the evening that I arrived, after having a rest and a shower, I walked from the desk in the foyer towards the exit, waving the key to the young lady behind the desk. She smiled and nodded but just as I made it to the door, she raised her hand to her open mouth and shook her head. So I wasn't allowed to take the key out with me but I was to leave it with her. She kept it under the desk and my head was spinning. So I left the bloody key and I walked towards the door that led out to the street, smiling and nodding and she was nearly beside herself at the hilarity of it all. I kept on walking. It was alright. It was okay – this time. And I left.

* * * * * * * * *

During my time in Japan, I had a continual aching pain in my left ankle. In fact, I had it there the year before and some time before that but it was getting worse. It made things a little arduous because of the amount of walking around that I was doing and I like to walk about places so it did irritate me. I had gone through the process of trying to find out what it was and after seeking the great sagacity of members belonging to the medical profession, I took tablets that are intended to subdue the effects of gout. And it was that condition I thought I had whilst walking around and at times in near agony. Yet, a couple years after this period of time that I am writing about I discovered, purely by chance, that I have flat feet. Yes, dropped arches were the problem all the while. I will tell you that it has been remedied by having an insole placed in my shoe. See? Interesting? That's me.

Anyway, getting back to Kyoto in the spring of 2003. A fine rain caused the automatic reaction for a tree of umbrellas to be opened and a pleasing sight in all their shapes, designs and colours I felt it to be. I walked to the nearby subway station, now having a map of Kyoto that was written in English. I had bought it in the hotel. There was no negotiation involved, it was easy. I put the required amount of money in a vending machine and chose the map that was written in a language that made sense to me. I would be able to navigate my wandering around this pleasant city. Again the railway staff were helpful so I found the train and platform or track that I needed and headed for 'down town' Kyoto. Although getting late, I noticed that a large amount of the passengers were travelling from work.

An Unlikely Fooligan

Well, I made a guess at that but I was sure it was the case and later that night I found out that I was right. I stepped off at a station and spent the next five minutes trying to get out of it. The tracks seemed to be deep underground and there were a lot of corridors and stairs to walk down and climb before the darkened night-time air that was filled with traffic noise and punctuated with neon rays came into being. And I was there, I had made it, I was outside, in the world of Kyoto. One word came to mind; shopping.

The wide pavements of a main street that I walked down were covered by a large canopy affair that kept the rain off the commodity hunters who tracked in a seemingly infinite trail that was a congealed body mass, each person separate but part of the insatiable mass. Designer bags that carried designer goods were in abundance but now their exclusivity had been diminished because so great were their preponderance within the possessed press that squawked and moved as one and I was feeling weak and overwhelmed with the profusion of it all. I walked past windows having signs and writing on them that presumably, gave directions to sub and even further sub labyrinths of glitzy burrows containing even more outlets that sell – sell – sell – sell – sell and I had to stand to the side of the pavement, disengaging myself from the caterpillar like procession. Near sickening thoughts to the future of this planet's resources came to mind and of how can it possibly sustain this feeding frenzy?

I escaped the breathlessness of the babbling stream and took what I mistakenly thought would be refuge through a doorway that led to an odd looking stairwell. It was like being in the back of a warehouse, the barren decor conflicted with the high velocity sound and colour that drove the consumerist wheel and in a way I felt that it was like discovering part of the mechanism that isn't seen by the consumer, yet is an essential part of it all. In fact, a part making up the bulk of the industry of sell and it is here, in this derelict environment where men and women spend their working days in jobs that pay a wage that couldn't possibly sustain the bare fundamentals of just living, let alone indulge in the participation of acquiring the goods or sharing the aspirations that those on the front end of this relationship share. The dust and grease on the lift that carries the goods and the people that handle them is in contrast to the customer elevator that is decorative and enticing. There is the smiling face of the woman who stands in the lobby greeting the customers, all neatly turned out in her uniform but if one looks, closely mind to see through the facade, one will see that her smile is fixed into a face that shows the dust and weariness that exists behind the highly polished and brightly lit presentation of products.

I made an effort to escape this spangled jungle and eventually my effort paid off when I crossed a main road and became lost in an area of very narrow streets that were lined with what I had imagined traditional Japanese buildings to be like. They were small and most of them were restaurants and the like. They were expensive and everyone was Japanese looking. I had read that this city and maybe it was that area, was still a place where the Geisha girl could be spotted. I understand that there are tourist arrangements where people can book a session with a Geisha or probably someone dressed as one and have tea served to them. I did indeed see a few women dressed in the traditional costumes and I must admit I stared at them. I wanted to know more. I was in a foreign land and it's interesting to see difference.

'Geisha'. This is the term commonly used by outsiders. The face is painted, mask white and the clothing is incongruous when compared to the modern dress of women where shackles and bondage have been shrugged off. Here the tightly bound, meek and deferential woman-girl-child aiding the needs of man is seen as a principal Japanese image. Although it is a minority activity, the concealment as represented by the pallid mask is not, I felt, central to Japanese culture. The giggling timid feminine graciousness with a display of excessive attention to man has become expected behaviour for woman to perform by foreigners when thinking of Japanese women. The Geisha exemplifies that dutiful, meticulous and humble self, offering light nervous laughter as the man demonstrates his wishes, thoughts or actions. Yet the girl-child-woman giggle cutie is no dumb waitress, for she also offers serenity, trust and security; a sanctuary that is a place of solace, beauty and refinement away from the combative environment that is the world of commerce. Inscribed as deeply into the face of Japanese culture as much as the tattoo is impregnated into the skin of a Yakuza member, this painted lady follows detailed attention to tradition in the arts, ceremonies, dress, etiquette and all the other stuff that goes with the thing. She is an ocean, being calm and soothing for she is teacher, mummy, sister, girlie, woman, lusted after and also respected – an aesthetic having an important function in grounding and justifying the might and mood of this powerful nation and people.

But Geisha Gladys is on the way out. The average age of retirement is fifty and her chances of survival can be seen as more fragile than the delicate refinement shown in her smile or hand movement. I have read that there are maybe a thousand of the graceful kimono clad beauties left, not even a handful in comparison to the population and nowhere near enough make up a handful in one of Riki Shi's big palms – and with his other hand the great man will wipe away the tears as he thinks of those tea house songs the Geisha whined out whilst playing the three stringed instrument called a shamisen and the way she turns her body as she does her fan dance.

An apprentice geisha is called a Maiko. Yes, Maggie Maiko learns the rules and etiquette and the present ones may well be some of the last who have made such a significant contribution to tradition as TLOTRS dilutes from its original recipe and goes through the process of economic and cultural osmosis and becomes part of the happy global village, a place where identification is shaped and designed by marketing executives in trans-national companies. Tokyo Joe, Kyoto Kate and Hiroshima Harry, along with all their values and artefacts, are being dragged into the open field and their belongings laid bare in the great car boot sale because this is where all of us refugees now exist. The oscillating individual rummaging through the rubbish on the trestle tables, all having our snouts in offerings given by the monopolised economy. There is a vagueness, a sameness, an urgency and a fear and security forces will expand as the political prisoner exists, the extremist, like a ghost unable to tolerate and conform and has a constant presence in the news that we are given and so lives within our minds, giving an aching but remote hunch that all is not as it should be. I watched the diminutive woman in her silk costume shuffle her small stepping trot across the uneven street surface, her tiny manicured hand holding a small umbrella that looked more like a petite parasol above her perfect head, protecting her creation from a drizzling rain that couldn't understand or spell the word Geisha but only does what it does and it did.

I toured the tiny streets, looking through the slatted windows at Japanese looking diners. The prices were exorbitant and I was tired and not in the mood to stand in a lounge area of a cramped restaurant and drink beer so I headed for the station with intentions of going back to the area where the hotel was. The pavements were swamped with people, mainly cheerful looking people and for a race that are often perceived to be quiet and robot like, they made a lot of noise. There was far more laughter than I heard on the busy streets back home. Laughing seems to come easy and often at the obvious which was lucky for me because my slapstick humour went down well and it was all that I had. I made it to the station, found out what track I needed and then stood on the platform feeling the warm gush of air coming from the tunnel drying my wet clothes. The train whooshed through that tunnel as if chasing the warm air and it stopped right in front of me, the doors opened and I stepped in. It was ten thirty at night and the train was quite full even at that time. A man burst into the carriage, just making it as the doors were closing. Steadying himself, he made his way to a vacant seat that was only a short distance but he approached it as if he had to leap over a furnace of burning oil. A young woman wearing a miniskirt made room for him in the next seat, moving to one side but not taking her eyes away from the page in the book that she was reading. I looked at the man. There was blood on the front of his suit jacket and down his white shirt and strips of antiseptic plaster tape ran from his forehead down his nose and across his cheek in two tracks. The blood was coagulating beneath the transparent tape. He adjusted his glasses and peered drunkenly through the lenses, his eyes not settling on anyone or anything. He just was. Nobody took any notice. They just were. Heads in books, waiting, staring at the ground, a tired carriage of waiting people. I was aware of a rancid smell, probably sweat that had dried and was ingrained into the carriage after yet again a long and heated day and there was this man sitting there, taking his place in the presentation of waiting, except he was covered in blood for Christ's sake. He looked like he had been thrown down the escalators, head first. He was almost an advert for raw meat. There might have been the odd quick glance at him from other people in the carriage but that was it. It was as if he hadn't entered. Then it hit me. It was as if we all hadn't arrived here. I felt a surge of trepidation as I thought about our existence but cast such thoughts aside of seeing us as little more than microbes responding with an unconscious instinct to survive. I saw that some people were looking at me and I thought of the year before when the fooligan came into existence and the mechanism that constructed the fooligan type; the brute with piggy eyes and piggy skin and piggy build, his pink outer casing embellished with tattoos, his behaviour foreign and dysfunctional. He occupied a place in the Japanese psyche. It was an image. It was created, bracketed and ready to be addressed in the appropriate manner, if need be with a physical force, a coercion that 'Master Fooligan' had never felt in the land where he comes from because the Japanese are not weak people and will not bow to those unworthy of respect. But it never happened because the fooligan was an invention. Just another example of how many of our perceptions are merely fabrications and in our abstracted way we follow a course that can indeed give us misleading thoughts to what we really are. I stopped myself. I wasn't even drunk. In fact, I hadn't had one drink.

I nodded at the bloodied man and offered what I imagined to be an all knowing and empathising smile but it was ignored. I nodded at him again, raising my eyebrows at the irony of life and all that but again, nothing. He just sat there and we all just sat there.

* * * * * * * * *

I stepped off the train and realised it wasn't the station I wanted. It meant more walking and it was raining and the pain that I thought at that time was gout seized like an aching wrap around my left ankle and I started to copy the way Japanese women walk, the way that they drag their heels giving a distinctive shuffle sound as they take short steps, performed quite quickly with the heel of the shoe dragging on the ground. With me it was different. I just lumbered along letting the heels of my shoes drag on the ground whilst the fine rain dampened my clothes that had only just dried. I walked around for a short while, passing large temples. This is what Kyoto is famous for although they were shut to the public at that time of night. The dark trees created a dense cloak of shadows over the pavement. It became relatively quiet considering that the main roads were only yards or metres away and then I found that I had walked in a circle. I couldn't find a place that I wanted to go into for a beer. There were lots of little bar lounges, some having American retro signs, mainly with hardly anyone in them. I took a look in one of them. A young lady, attractive of course, was sitting behind the bar gazing at the people who were passing by and who would sometimes momentarily stop to look though the window but then only to continue on their way. I decided not to stay but find the station and get a train to the area where my hotel was.

I became lost as I looked for the station and felt that it was useless trying to ask anyone. I was tired and they were tired so I made my way to a busy junction and from there, I sighted a red light on top of a tower that I recognised. It was a significant landmark.

I took shelter in a bar from unremitting rain that was becoming tedious. It was as if the rain itself was bored with its constant drizzle. The place I had stepped into was a city bar affair, not what I like and too expensive, of course. I ordered a beru, a large one. There was nothing of interest in the place. It had a youngish clientele whom I imagined to be students and young professionals. I was probably wrong but designer clothing of the casual range and not much else didn't stir my interest. The rain welcomed me back to Kyoto as I exited the bar and having the red light on top of the tower in my sights, I walked in that direction knowing, hopefully, that the hotel was in that area. I reached the tower and after spending a minute standing outside the thing trying to find out what it was, I kept on walking. The ache in my left ankle kept reminding me that I would never be a top class athlete. I walked down a long avenue that indeed took me to an area that I recognised but of course, one can get confused. What with it being unfamiliar and me having done a lot of walking around unfamiliar places during the day, it's easy to mistake a street for being a street in a completely different city that one was in earlier in the day.

Anyway, I found the main road that the station was on and I walked up to the hotel. On reaching the entrance of the hotel, I stopped and turned around. I crossed the road and walked down a narrow road that led into maze of narrow streets. Here, just apart from modern Japan with its large concrete architecture and noise were quiet little residential streets, some looking too narrow for a car to be driven down. I passed by the small houses. The lights were on inside them and I wondered what kind of television programmes people were watching before calling it a night, going to bed, getting up in the morning and leave this quaint 'old Japan' setting to join the chaotic charge of modernity that exists just around the corner from where they live. I imagined a young boy or a girl, very young, maybe two or three years of age, resting peacefully in a little bed in a room in one of the neat little houses, a teddy bear or favourite toy nestling all comfortable and safe by his or her side; earlier on mum had read a story or maybe sung a lullaby in a tone that is different from what I am used to in the land that I come from but has the same meaning. I looked at the bottles of gas standing outside the back of the houses, a fuel that gives energy. I realised that I was getting wet and there on the corner of the street was a red lantern hanging outside a door way – a bar! It seemed a strange place to see a bar but then why not? The red lantern places were local bars but the area was so quiet, in fact it was silent. I couldn't imagine that there would be anyone in there.

I was wrong. The door that one opened to enter was the traditional type. It was a sliding door having panels and seemed to be of a flimsy construction. I poked my head though the door for a quick look before fully entering and was surprised that I had discovered a parlour of vibrancy. It was small and self-contained. Nearly all eyes that weren't engaged in conversation or thoughts that absorbed, turned as the door slid open and there was Mr Foreigner. I could tell by the reaction that not many of my type came to this little establishment. I closed the door behind myself, sliding it shut and in doing so, shutting out the fine rain that swirled in soft wire-like bushel shapes. I turned and looked at the bar counter which wasn't very far from the door as the place wasn't big. From where I stood, there were three large tables to my left that had seating around them but in that Japanese way of having to sit more or less on the floor. Not good for the portly gentleman or those with arthritic joints in their lower limbs. A narrow space ran in front of the counter and at the far end of that space, there were the toilets to the left. On my right, next to the door, was a machine. It was some kind of game I suppose and standing around it were a bunch of young people, looking like college student types but I could have been wrong. The place had a homely feel about it. I liked it. There was a gentle and happy hubbub of noise.

It was late and the patrons in this content little place were well oiled. I approached the bar counter but before I could order my drink, I saw that the man behind it was watching me with dramatic intensity. As I've said, I had found a lot of Japanese people to enjoy slapstick fun and here was a man with a bandanna tied around his head, having coal black eyes that could pierce stone or steel and holding a large and sharp looking chopper in his right hand – and it was pointing at me.

"Eh," he said it in an abrupt way, spitting it out just like those Japanese soldiers do in the films that I saw as a child. "Beer please. Beru – large one please – jumbo." I gestured with my hands that I wanted a large beer but the man with the kamikaze look didn't move. He didn't flinch. His eyes fixed onto me as if he was trying to clear images that existed in a deep cave somewhere in his mind. He reminded me of Master Samurai, only far more severe and fierce looking. I gave him some time. I nodded and I smiled, nodding in a way that told him that he was right, that he was correct in whatever it was that he was thinking. And eventually he too nodded but only slightly, no way near the ceremonial Japanese bow. This was just a nod that barely made it to the outside world, the real intent having been inner reflection. "Jumbo," he said suddenly and he pointed the chopper that looked like an axe at my midriff area. "You," he said in a way that was a command, "you are jumbo." I looked down at myself and then up, slowly, in a kind of straight-faced way. "Thanks," I said and I pushed my stomach out further and puffed out my chest and I made my shoulders wider and wider still until I could hardy breath and it was nearly hurting. I was on holiday, for Christ's sake. Isn't this the normal way to behave? The man with the axe dropped his pose of stern interrogator, the hard edge fell from his eyes and he turned in a half circle, nearly giggling like a little girl but then he stopped all of a sudden. He pointed the axe at me and the hard character had returned. "You, beer – jumbo beru." And then he nearly folded again in the giggle routine. He turned and looked at me. The essence that makes a smile splashed across his face but without the smile itself. "Jumbo – you, Jumbo!" There it was again, that word. Jumbo. I was beginning to understand how children at school felt when having to endure this kind of thing. I'm not going down the road of saying that I felt bullied or intimidated. I smiled, an all embracing smile, open and big enough for everyone and their friends to throw their remarks into because it was empty and could never be filled because there was nothing to fill. But it was sufficient and I didn't have many or any other options at hand if I wanted to partake in a bit of social interaction.

I looked at the man and grinned and I looked about myself. There were a few people looking at me so I nodded and smiled at them and they reciprocated by smiling and nodding back. The man behind the bar snapped an order at a young man, who was also working behind the bar, in a manner that told me that the young man was subordinate in their bar work relationship. The young man placed the beer in front of me and I put the money in the palm of his hand after he had spelled out to me how much it was in a slow and deliberate mime. He said it five or six times in a way that one sees an adult trying to communicate with a very young child with severe hearing problems. I noticed that there was a tall Indian/Asian looking man standing at the bar. I nodded at him and he nodded back. He appeared to have a friendly nature and I was to find out later that indeed he did. The young man who was working behind the bar also had a bandanna tied around his head but his head was round and his face was chubby so it didn't give the image that I had when as a child seeing the cartooned faces of Japanese airman and soldiers in comics. The young man started to tap a rhythm with his hands and he looked at me and smiled. The drumming was his approach at communication. I smiled and nodded a gesture that said what he was doing is good. So he did it again and I drummed a beat on the bar, following it with a fast roll. The young man looked at me, his eyes widening a little in recognition that I could play the drums and I grinned and did it again. He tried to talk to me about it but it was useless. We couldn't communicate. Through clumsy mime we established that he didn't play the drums or any other instrument but he liked music and that I do play the drums. He went on to try and explain about a concert or festival that he had been to or was going to. I wasn't sure but he played some air guitar and this caught the attention of the main man behind the counter who shot the young man a look that might as well have been a bullet. Although it was laced with humour, it said that the young man was a lost cause. I swiftly pulled my phrase book out and asked if they were father and son. This set off an immediate cry of denial from both of them and much laughter. The young man explained to the man that I played the drums and I did a drum roll on the counter to substantiate his claim. But this didn't impress the man. He just stared at me and nodded and like Master Samurai, there was a hidden glow in his set expression and a distant shimmer within his black eyes that sought and appreciated fun.

The young man and I continued to exchange looks and nods as he emptied and filled the rice machine, chopped vegetables and cooked the little skewers of meat. This is the norm in these little Japanese bars, in the local bars. Food is the customary accessory when having a drink. I watched the young man take a cigarette from his mouth, blow smoke away from the food that he was preparing, place the cigarette on the edge of the counter where he was working and continue to put an order together. The smoking behind the bar thing was common. I smiled inwardly at what response that would evoke in certain quarters back home in the clinically hygienic, bureaucratically over burdened world where there is an industry created for 'food hygiene professionals' where consultancies vie to swallow grants paid for by beleaguered taxpayers and the whole thing reeks of contradictions and hypocrisy and is proven to be incompetent, ineffective and a failure as the evidence shows that food poisoning is on the increase. It's common sense that having a cigarette dangling from one's mouth will not give anyone food poisoning. I was told by a few British people that they don't know of anyone getting food poisoning in Japan, that was from my friends and a chap I was speaking to who was working in Japan. All the constraints, restrictions and requirements shape up to be a hollow call when one considers the poor quality meat bought illegally by proprietors of the various take-away places in Britain, imported from where it shouldn't have been, in places having filthy conditions and then stored and prepared when back in Britain in disgusting conditions that are infected with creatures that shouldn't be around food that people are going to eat. Mix that in with reusing very old oil and putting food in containers to use the following day and the day after and a cat and mouse game exists between the authorities and the proprietors of this horrible and dangerous cuisine.

And when I have a cynical moment, I think that the situation suits both parties. One, the authorities, for all the jobs and careers and training consultancy positions that it creates and two, the establishments themselves as the proprietors are able to trade in a country that allows such deplorable conditions. All they have to do is avoid the inspectors and if caught, just pay a fine and at worst start up another company under a different name. You see? There is no real intent in doing anything about it. There is no will from the society as a whole to sort it out. And it might sound strange – I don't even smoke cigarettes – but I had a good feeling seeing the young man smoke his cigarette when thinking of the preposterousness of the sham back home of having laws to protect people.

I looked up and the main man behind the counter was watching me. I woke myself from my thoughts and raised my glass, "Kampai," I said which is 'cheers' in Japanese. The man took a second before he responded. He laughed and pointed the axe at me and he turned and picked up a glass that I took was containing sake and raised it. "Kampai," he said. He took a sip of the drink and laughed. "Kampai – Jumbo!" And he laughed some more. The black coals that were his eyes now ablaze with life's energy. I tipped my glass upwards, pouring its contents down my throat in one draft. This made the man gawp at me as he struck a stage-like pose, his mouth open in wonderment at my mighty feat. Then he pointed his axe, cleaver, chopper, hefty kitchen knife or whatever it's called, at me and laughed, again nearly folding in upon himself which was his way and he raised his hand to his mouth to suppress a mock outburst at seeing such behaviour. I made a big show of wiping my mouth and ordering another and as I mimed the act of a big man wanting more drink, I noticed that just along the bar, to my right on the other side of the tall Indian looking man, was a man who was watching me and he also wanted to join in the fun. He was a tough looking chap, not big and bulky but powerfully built. On taking a closer look, I saw the history of this man's life written in scar tissue, misshapen bones and an ear that was irretrievably twisted due to being damaged, probably because this man had been or maybe still was, a boxer or that type of thing. He had a friendly way about him but me being a coward and in my defence rightly being a bit careful about my conduct in unknown territory, I checked myself a little. I nodded to the man and smiled. He returned the smile and stood up from his stool. He stepped towards me and shook my hand. It had enough power to open a cast iron safe in any high street bank. But he didn't push his strength and I acknowledged his power, giving him a nod that I should imagine is universally recognised by men in bars and similar situations. He gave me a friendly pat on my shoulder and I returned the act that was a gesture to make contact when verbal communication was an impossibility. The man indicated that I was a big man, although he meant it in a way that he knew I was just clowning and having a joke because it is obvious to anyone who knows anything about the world of fighters and the like that I am certainly not from that world. The man had a friendly face yet looking hard enough to butt a bullet train off its rails; he was from that world. I have to say that although there are many references to me being big in this story, I am in fact not that big. It's just that in Japan I come across as being bigger than where I come from and I have been told that I can project a presence that can give people the impression that I am lager than I actually am. I hope that I've explained myself clearly.

I threw a mock and it was a very mock, punch in very slow motion towards the man's shoulder and he parried it and lowered his head in the classic fighter stance. I grinned and so did he and the axe man behind the counter intervened, miming a situation that looked as if he was trying hug and strangle himself. The axe man kept repeating a word, struggling to find a translation that I would understand and all the while looking at the tall Indian looking man. Eventually the tall Indian looking man leaned towards me. "He's a wrestler," he said and he nodded at the tough looking man. He said it in very clear English. It stopped me as if a giant hand had appeared through the clouds. It also made me think to be a little more mindful of my behaviour as I immediately lost the feeling of being a complete alien and that my conduct could now be questioned. The clarity of the words that he had spoken seemed to shift the woolliness of my situation and it was as if there had been an adjustment to the focus on the camera that I was looking through. The bar with its activities became defined and I was more conscious of myself within it. "You speak English?" I said to the tall Indian looking man. He made a sign with his hand as though saying, "Yes but maybe not that great," and he shrugged in a modest manner. We had a chat and I went on to tell him that it doesn't take long for me to feel disorientated, meaning that it takes just a day of being amongst people where there is a different tone to an indecipherable language.

The man told me his name which I have forgotten and we shook hands. He was a polite and intelligent man and I could see that he enjoyed the absurdity that exists in life. He gave a wry smile to my venting and we talked a little about Japanese culture and the way of things. He was from Malaysia and had relatives in Jersey, that small isle that has crumbled off the south coast of England, although now being closer to France which offers tax breaks and clement weather in comparison to many parts of Britain. During the course of the night, he told me that he worked in Japan and the bar that we were in was his local. He told me that things were getting tighter at work and there were demands to work later, till past eleven at night and that's when you get in at eight in the morning. The salary men, as they're called, will stay as long as they think they have to although the Malayan man told me that they don't do a lot. It's just part of the game to be seen being there but now he has to suffer this because the foreign company that he works for has changed his contract. He now has to work to the same conditions that indigenous workers do. In short, he's lost the benefits of better money, shorter hours, longer holidays, expenses and support in having accommodation paid for. It prompted the question. "Why do you stay here?" I asked him. He told me that things were stretched where he came from and that he did have a good deal when he came to Japan, especially for a non-European and that he'll see what happens but at the moment that's the cards he's been dealt. I spoke to him about the World Cup being held in Japan the previous year and of my experience of being asked if

I was fooligan by people. We talked about the media and of how it generated the imagery and expectations of what an English football fan was. We had a laugh about it and he said to me, "You're an unlikely fooligan."

And then I saw that the wrestler was still looking at me. Maybe he had been watching me all the time that I had been talking to the Malayan man. And there also was the axe man. He too was watching me and he was nodding his head in a way that said, "That's right – that's right Jumbo, you're in our world now," and a grin hid beneath his fiery visage.

I told my friend, the Malayan man, that the bar had a good feel about it and seemed to attract some good characters. He agreed, telling me that it was a good humoured bar having its regular locals and that the proprietor kept a good place for those who came in for a drink and to relax. He introduced me to the owner, the axe man. His name was Master Fuji. It was explained to me that it was a cultural thing, having its roots in the Shinto belief system to name a person after a significant and unique facet of the natural world, like a mountain for example, as representing spirituality. The axe man made a shape of what was intended to be a mountain and then pointed to himself. "Fuji-san," as Mount Fuji is known in Japanese and he smiled and quite interestingly for the first time since I had entered the bar, I noticed a change in his bearing. He said his name with pride but it was said with a little reticence at what my response might be, reminding me of a provincial person feeling embarrassed but proud of their ways when being visited or questioned by a person from the big city as if knowing that their ways are quaint and might be scoffed at by the fast talking city slickers who race in the fast lane. Anyway, that's how I read it. I was sure that I was right because Master Fuji lowered his chin, just a little and the fire quelled from his eyes, just a touch, and they looked at me, waiting for a response. I was sure that a slight blush shaded the skin on his face as his manner quietened.

I nodded. "Fuji-san," I said as I picked up my glass and toasted the great mountain and I said, "Kampai." Master Fuji turned, the life now fully lit and blaring in his face. He picked up his drink and said, "Fuji-san." I toasted the great rock yet again and so did Master Fuji and the wrestler joined in for here was a man who liked life and fun. Master Fuji walked in a circle, laughing and then he picked up his axe and pointed it at me, "You – you, Jumbo!" He toasted 'Jumbo' and I joined him and so did the wrestler and I said to my translator friend, 'Jumbo! I didn't reckon for this – an unlikely fooligan indeed.' He was a man who had a sense of irony and dry wit. He chinked my glass and said very quietly, "To Jumbo."

The wrestler was with a woman who was a fair bit younger than he was. He nudged her as he laughed and she smiled politely at me. I raised my glass and chinked his, then hers and then Master Fuji's. The wrestler introduced himself and then his girlfriend. She said her name in a tone that was like fine china and could break at any time and here she was, having a relationship with a man who was as durable as an axle on a freight train. As she told me her name, he offered me her hand. It was small and slender. It was cool to the touch. It was like holding an orchid. The wrestler told me his name and again he shook my hand. That same hand of mine that had just held the soft skinned hand with its delicate structure was now being gripped by granite with a course leather coating. We raised our drinks and smiled but not a lot else was being said. The Malayan man grinned as he oversaw the proceedings that were taking place before him. After some joking around with Master Fuji where we gripped each other's hands and he threatened me with his axe in that over dramatic stage posturing that is common in TLOTRS, I became aware of someone speaking to me from along the bar. It was one of the youngsters by the machine. They were all looking at me and smiling as one of them said, "Beckham," and he nodded his head and repeated the seemingly ubiquitous word in that land, "Beckham." He pointed at me and although I'm pretty stupid, believe me I am not that mad, not even with the delirious state brought on by travel, confusion and tiredness to know that he didn't think that I was the tall good looking one who has near on completed the feat of world domination simply by having a pleasant smile and character. "Beckham!" I said in mock derision and I shook my head making a deprecatory gesture on hearing the name of the hallowed one. And this ignited a loud response from the group by the machine. They rose in spontaneous laughter, some grabbing hold of the one next them because it was too much for them.

Opposite to the group by the machine were three office girls sitting around one of the tables next to the entrance and dressed in that corporate uniform of a dark blue dress suit and white blouse. They giggled and laughed at the fun and I thought maybe at some remarks that might have been made about the outsider who didn't understand what was being said. Maybe there were no remarks and it was just a bit of fun because that is how it felt. There was no feeling of there being any sarcasm or nastiness. The young women showed signs of having had a few drinks, being all glassy eyed and rubber limbed. The empty bottles of sake, the Japanese wine, on their table gave evidence to having a drink after work turning into getting drunk after work. They, like the others in the bar, seemed a cheery and friendly bunch. I raised my glass at them and said, "Kampai," and they raised their glasses and returned the toast, all nearly shrieking, "Kampai" as one even though two of them didn't notice that their glasses were empty. Then on realising that they were, there was the lunging and grabbing at handbags that had slunk under the table and eyes that couldn't focus passed over money and sent information to a brain that couldn't count as they put their money together to buy some more sake. The wrestler thought it hilarious when I raised my glass to the young women and he nudged his girlfriend. This was something that he did a lot in a gesture to involve her in the merriment. I figured that if this is the normal state of affairs, she would do well to have a little protection around her ribs, maybe something like a nicely fitting steel plate because I for one wouldn't relish the prospect of going out for a drink and knowing that old granite face, as nice and kind as he was, would be digging me in the ribs every few minutes to find out if I knew what was going on.

I turned and smiled at the Malayan man at the fun and manner of the people in the bar. The Malayan man was an observer. He too was an outsider and standing to the side of what was happening in his quiet and polite manner. He seemed to be accepted in his role as the decorous bystander. I spoke to him about the readiness that many Japanese people have for a bit of larking about and of how it is communicated in slapstick humour. He told me that I was lucky that I was an outgoing person because I would experience far more contact with Japanese people than most who visit the country for just a couple of weeks.

Since entering the bar I had noticed and at times watched the group of people sitting around the table next to where the Malayan man and I were standing. There were three middle-aged women. I later found out that they were in their late fifties and a slim man in his early thirties. What I had noticed about this man was that he had china blue eyes. At first sighting I just thought that was the way it is but then I checked myself and after a closer look, I realised that he was wearing blue contact lenses. The whole gang of them were woozy with the drink. There was plenty of laughing and leaning across the table, pointing fingers in mock accusation and then falling about with laughter. The women kept looking at me and I raised my glass and went through the ritual of saying, "Kampai." They rolled into one another, raising their glasses and laughing some more. They were doing better than their male comrade. It looked as if the end of the night was fast falling in on him as a docile smile rested at a disjointed angle on his face giving the image of blurred stupidity. One of the women managed to disengage herself from the table. What with it being so low, it would be difficult enough in normal times but now that she was well oiled, it was a cumbersome affair. She wanted to speak to me and she took hold of my arm to steady herself. The Malayan man smiled expectantly at the probable comic amusement that was forthcoming. The woman tried out her broken English on me but it was so broken that I found it difficult to decipher the faltering fragments. It was frustrating and she, because of the drink I should imagine, thought that her communication was more lucid than it actually was. In fact it was a patchwork of a language delivered with an intonation that rose from shrill to guttural flat. The phrase book would have been useless at this time of night in this bar. She was a friendly person and I could sense with good intentions. The Malayan man's body gave a little. It was an involuntary shift as he laughed whilst remaining respectful. He told me that the woman and her two friends were Girl Guides and that they came from Tokyo. The women were having a short break in Kyoto. There had been some kind of Scouts and Guides symposium and the man with them was a Buddhist priest. He had been showing them around the temples earlier in the day. The woman was showing me a cross that was around her neck as she repeated the name, 'Jesus'. The Malayan man told me that the women were Roman Catholics.

The story was that they were in Kyoto for a short trip and they had contacted a Buddhist priest or monk who was the man with the blue contact lenses and due to the drink was weaving around because his legs had lost any semblance of feeling and being part of his body. He stayed upright by doing a movement that looked like he was trying to stand still whilst standing on a water bed or a bouncy castle. The priest had kindly offered his services of acting as a guide, showing the ladies around the temples and giving them information on the origins of the temples and details of the Buddhist belief. They had decided to drop off into this bar about four in the afternoon for a rest and have something to eat and maybe a drink. Over eight hours later this unusual group had soaked up the

culture and sake with a driving enthusiasm and it looked likely that the Roman Catholic contingent in this little gathering was going to stay the course better than the solo Buddhist who performed that universal smile of a simpleton that let people know that they had drunk beyond their limit. He slowly closed and opened his eyes to reveal the weird sight of blue contact lenses.

I knocked back my beer with gusto which made the Girl Guide laugh. I ordered myself another, making a big show of wiping my mouth and pushing out my chest and stomach. This made the woman laugh some more and she held her hand to her mouth to suppress such a bold expression of laughter at another person. The woman took hold of one of her friend's arms and tried to pull her up. This roused the interest of the third woman and the priest. I made another show of striking a pose that was something between an American wrestler and a character from the silent films which sparked off the woman again to shiver with laughter and she gave me a playful slap on my shoulder. I put my arm around her shoulder and gave her a hug which caused the other two women to emit a near deafening cry of shrill laughter in an act of letting themselves go whilst also remaining staid and self-consciousness. This also caused the wrestler to explode into laughter and his girlfriend received another body jolting nudge in her ribs just to remind her what was going on. She shook on her stool graciously with a smile that might have been borne from obedience. The Girl Guide made a show of grabbing my arm and screeched words in my ear, laughing all the more and now the other two women were on their feet, standing close by with their hands over their mouths but the priest wasn't so animated. He was just hanging on for the ride.

My Malayan friend told me that the woman said she would use aikido on me and she made a play of twisting my arm and the wrestler was almost beside himself and he nearly made a move to intervene and show the woman how to perform the move correctly but his girlfriend, rather bashfully, held his arm as a signal for him to stay where he was which I was most grateful to her for. I turned to the bar and ordered a drink and as I went to pay for it, the Malayan man interjected and insisted that he bought this one for me. The women were becoming louder and wanted to know about London and if I was or still am, a scout. I told them that I had never been involved in such organisations because they wouldn't have suited my singular personality. I then made some remarks about Baden Powell and on mentioning his name, the three women grabbed at one another and let forth screeching sounds. It reminded me of teeny boppers engaging in a group hysterical response on seeing their idol walking down the street. Baden Powell, all these years later, the shorts wearing one with a penchant for sleeping in tents and gathering young people around a fire to sing 'team' songs together. I thought about the structure of the scouting organisation with the different names given to those with varying degrees of status and the importance of uniforms and badges that depict what achievements have been recognised by the all powerful system and of course, its emperor Baden Powell, overseeing the uniformity and welfare of his young charges as they break into divisions having a hierarchical pecking order signifying positions of power that is part of an intricate system that maintains group or pack order by regulating and disciplining themselves. I made an aside remark to my Malayan friend about the sometimes alleged murky image of the founder of scouting. He grinned but I held back from discharging defamatory comments to the women about their leader. They seemed too nice to turn things all sordid.

The wrestler wanted to join in the merriment and Master Fuji was watching over the proceedings. Every time I looked at him he raised the axe and nodded, pulling a face of chief prison officer. I tried to involve the priest and I mentioned his blue contact lenses. The priest was a friendly type and he told me where his temple was. My Malayan friend translated all this information. I told the priest that I have read a bit about Buddhism and that I found the philosophy to be interesting and also helpful but he was past having a conversation about guided meditation and impermanence especially as it had to be translated through a third person and one didn't need to have the knowledge of a Buddhist monk to experience a sense of the transitory. Ask anyone who gets drunk, all things are fleeting and usually gone tomorrow. Discarding efforts of having a chat about Buddhism, I reverted to simple 'Jumbo land' and joked with the priest or monk and the women – and then, well all things went a little lopsided. I asked the monk why he was wearing blue contact lenses but he made out that he wasn't – and I wouldn't let it rest and went on and about it. I said, "Old blue eyes, Frankie Sinatra himself," and the Girl Guides were shocked in a mock way, at my manners – and then – and then – I picked up the monk, turned him upside down and shook him to see if any coins would fall out of his pockets and also to see if his blue contact lenses would drop out. Listen, I know, I do know it's not the normal thing to do and I do realise that it is disrespectful but what with the banter and the language difficulty and it wasn't done with any malice or ill intent. On the contrary, it was done in an affectionate way and in the heat of things. Well, it caused heads to turn. The office girls shrieked and the woman who first spoke to me, playfully slapped my arm to reprimand me and the wrestler intervened, saying, 'No, no – priest – no.' I heard Master Fuji shout, "Jumbo!" Under the guidance of the wrestler, I settled the priest on his feet. He was smiling but the episode had unsettled his balance more than it was before. I realised that everyone in the bar was looking although with surprise rather than horror because it was within the boundary of good humour.

The wrestler had now involved himself with the group. Taking hold of my upper arm, he asked me to flex it which I did and he flexed his and I feigned a wrestling hold and he easily and with professional skill, dealt my clumsy attempt. It must have looked absurd and ridiculous as it always does in any bar anywhere when two middle-aged men carry on in such a way. What he lacked in verbal communication he made for with restoring order abilities, playing the part of a referee in a mock display of separating the monk and myself. The Malayan man shook his head slightly and the wrestler's girlfriend looked on, watching him with an expression on her face that said, 'It's too late now, he's off his lead'. The banter continued, mostly with no understanding to what was being said. It was the joining of a high spiritual agreement by people being brought together by slackened inhibitions caused by alcohol and an innate desire of wanting to reach out to people.

An Unlikely Fooligan

The wrestler pointed at me and called me Bruce Willis and then he burst into laughter as the Malayan man explained to him about my trip the previous year and the media hype of fooligans and of how I was marked out as being a fooligan by some people. It had become too late for the monk or priest and he called it a night. It had been a long day and I imagined him crawling under his futon that night with images of the day's events flashing through his mind, the traipsing around temples with fifty eight year old Girl Guides from Tokyo, comparing all that they saw and heard to their Roman Catholic religion and then to go into the bar, thinking that the day was nearly complete, with intentions of just stopping for a glass of wine with the ladies after a meal but it wasn't to be. Things became cluttered, the agenda went sailing through the window, it turned into a long drinking session that was punctuated with frenetic outbursts of animated laughter and then at the end, late at night, the odd image of a bald foreign man, things became aberrational, he was stout in build with a padded corporation, 'and that's right, he picked me up and turned me upside down'. Maybe the priest murmured to himself that he would leave it a little while before he returns to the bar.

The wrestler was putting a coat over his girlfriend's shoulders as he led her towards me. She had her hand extended, her lovely smile saying it all and I shook her slim hand as the wrestler spoke in breakneck speed to the Malayan man who told me that the wrestler had said that he is dropping off his girlfriend and then he was coming back to the bar. I watched the two of them leave. By now the priest had already gone. The Malayan man told me the priest only lived around the corner as did the wrestler and his girlfriend but they aren't living together at the moment. I spoke to him about the bar being a local's place and that I would like a similar one to be local to me where I come from. Whilst we were talking, the three girl guides showed no signs of slacking as another bottle of sake was ordered and purses were taken from bags. The three ladies showed me photographs of children, grown ups, older grown ups from a past time in Japan as their faces looked out at a new Japan through a sepia brown tinge and there were babies crawling across floors and a photograph of a dog looking up at the camera, acting all obedient in thinking he or she will get a treat for behaving well. I was given an insight into their families. Their faces creased and broke into laughter as I made comments that they didn't understand although some were translated by the overworked, never complaining Malayan man.

It was the Japan I was looking for. I liked their company. They were nice people. One of the women, the one that had first spoken to me, produced a small brass badge from her handbag. She showed it to me, moving it in her hand whilst giving me a commentary on the badge. The Malayan man stooped in, taking a close look at the badge. This one even seemed to have fazed him a little. I watched as his brow creased and he studied the little golden coloured badge and then he stepped back suddenly and laughed but then stopped

laughing as he looked at the woman and seemed to check his behaviour. He told me it was her Girl Guide badge and that it had been with her for many years. She looked proudly from the Malayan man to me and then down at the badge. The Malayan man showed me the initials on the front of the badge. J.G. S. There was also something written in Japanese in tiny writing underneath the initials. I didn't want to appear disrespectful but all the same I struck the pose of the scout, standing to attention, doing the salute with two fingers to the side of my head. This caused the woman to nearly shriek and she pulled at the other two women showing them what I was doing. They all raised their hands to their mouths, in between pointing to my fingers and the salute I was doing. The woman who was holding the badge reeled off words in excitement. To cut it short, they thought that I must have been a Boy Scout even if I said I wasn't because I knew the salute that they do. I tried to tell them that I wasn't but this had caused an animated commotion within the group of ladies. It was as if they had discovered something very important. The Malayan man told them that I wasn't a Boy Scout and that I had seen the salute done by others and that I was just larking about. Then he told me that the women thought that I was a good person even though I wasn't a scout. The woman holding the badge said something to her two friends and held the badge in front of herself in a formal fashion. This caused them to double over into raptures. The woman held the badge towards my face and spoke words that seemed to have a serious intent. The Malayan man nearly choked. He then told me that the women wanted to initiate me into the Guides and that they can do a ceremony in the bar and that I had the chance to become a Girl Guide even though I am a man. I grinned at this one but before I could respond the door to the bar slid open as if it was a lightweight curtain being drawn to one side and in walked the wrestler, all smiling and more relaxed now that he didn't have his girlfriend with him. He didn't want to miss out on any fun with the foreign man. His girlfriend was at home, probably strapping up her ribs and getting ready for the next night out. The wrestler ordered a beer and took no time getting himself involved in what was happening after being told by Master Fuji that the portly outsider, 'Jumbo' himself, was going to be made a Girl Guide in his bar. Master Fuji gave me a levelling look, his eyebrows raised, just a little. The wrestler wanted to take charge of the proceedings, telling me that I had to stand on the table. We checked it with Master Fuji and he gave the signal that it was permissible to do so. So, I clambered onto the low table and as I did this, I saw that it had drawn the attention of the three office girls. One of them pointed at me and of course her other hand was covering her mouth. It also drew attention from the young bunch around the machine. Being ready for some fun, they watched with grins on their faces as I was given instructions by the Japanese woman to stand in a position of giving a salute and repeat what she was saying, all of it in Japanese. This caused a gradual murmur of tittering that grew to open laughter and clapping from the patrons in the bar. God knows what I was saying. I thought that it was most probably something like, "I am a stupid fat man," or maybe worse but then I was judging by my own standards and remember these women were Girl Guides after all and they were very nice so maybe it wouldn't be the kind of trick that they would play on an unsuspecting foreigner.

Throughout the ceremony of admittance to the Japanese Girl Guides, the wrestler was hardly able to contain himself. I looked over at the bar and saw that the young man who worked alongside Master Fuji was looking on, an expression grasping for some kind of answer to what had happened to the foreign man who had entered the bar not that long ago. I was then asked to climb down from the table and the woman pinned the badge on my chest to rousing applause, cheers and laughter from the people in the bar. The wrestler reeled backwards, slapping my back with what felt like an iron bar but was only the flat of his hand. I heard the word, 'Jumbo' exclaimed loudly. It was Master Fuji. He narrowed his eyes and pointed his axe at me. Tightening his mouth into a thin cruel line, he put the axe down and came from behind the bar carrying two bottles of sake. He said something that caused some of the youngsters by the machine to twist their bodies and laugh out disbelieving cries. The Malayan man lowered his head towards mine. I had noticed that during the ceremony he was smiling from the side of his mouth as he witnessed this unlikely scene. He told me that the owner of the bar wanted to bless the ceremony with a toast. Glasses were handed out and as the sake was poured, the wrestler kept wrapping his arm around my shoulder and I thought to myself that his girlfriend, although appearing dainty and feminine must be a lot tougher than she looks if that's some kind of affectionate cuddle. Glasses were given to the patrons in the bar and I felt that the youngsters found it hard to believe that Master Fuji was in such good spirits and being so generous. Under the orders of Master Fuji, everybody raised their glasses and said something as well as 'Kampai'.

The place settled and through the linguistic abilities of my Malayan friend, the woman who gave me the badge told me where she lived in Tokyo and she wanted to know all about me. At the end of every sentence that I said, she would turn to her friends and tell them what I was saying and they would nod their heads in thoughtful concentration. And time was getting on, the good people who were in the bar had things to do in the morning. The youngsters made a move, bidding farewell. One of them called out the name 'Beckham' to me. I made some remark that caused the young man to buckle in laughter. It wasn't a very funny remark but then it was late and there had been alcohol and it was Japan. Just as I was preparing myself to leave, Master Fuji came out from behind the counter shouting out what sounded like orders and he secured the door to the bar shut. The Malayan man told me that Master Fuji wanted to have an after hours drink. He put some bowls of rice and a few bottles of sake on one of the low tables and he pointed at me as he spoke in his guttural way of firing out words that sounded like a rapid command. I heard the word Jumbo amongst the other words that he was saying. The Malayan man told me that Master Fuji wanted to have a talk with me. I looked at my interpreter. He raised his eyebrows, telling me that Master Fuji was a character, which I had noticed and even if people didn't want to stay and relax and have a drink and something to eat – they had to. So, the drinks were poured and the rice and bits and pieces were out and there were a few toasts made. 'Kampai' was the common denominator and Master Fuji pointed at me and spat out the word, 'Jumbo!'

With help from my Malayan friend, Master Fuji told me a bit about himself, what time he had to be up in the morning, the very long hours that he works in the bar and that he was born in the area of Kyoto where we now were. He wanted to know about me, where I came from and that other world. He was interested to know about my travels in Japan, he wanted to know what I thought of things and as the Malayan man interpreted what I was saying, Master Fuji watched me carefully, nodding thoughtfully, his eyes secured on me and sometimes his expression would soften and he nodded more deeply. He was a good man. Of course I didn't know him but from what I gathered by watching him, I felt him to be one of life's good characters. He makes the place that we have our journey in a better place to be. The sake and the food were on the house, a treat given by our host, Master Fuji. His young assistant sat red eyed with tiredness on a stool away from the table that we were sitting at. It was time to leave. We all made our way to the door. As I shook Master Fuji's hand, he wanted to know if I would be visiting his bar before I left. It was translated by the Malayan man that I would be dropping in the following night and then I would be off to Tokyo.

We stood in the narrow street outside the bar, the office girls giggling good humouredly and unable to gain a stable footing between them. Then we all walked up the street together but before we proceeded on our way, the Malayan man went around the side of the bar and returned with his push bike. He told me that he cycles to the bar. I tried to give one of the office girls a ride on the crossbar of the bike and lifted her off the ground. She was heavier than I thought she would be and I clowned around. It reminded me of a bunch of people leaving a pub in the countryside, having bumpkin fun, unsophisticated, yet here we were in Kyoto, a buzzing high tech city in Japan. I like that kind of thing, nothing pretentious. We made our way to the high street, stood on the street corner and chatted. Except with me it was only the Malayan man who understood what I was a saying. We bid our farewells and there were hugs from the office girls and before pointing me in the direction where my hotel was, the Malaya man told me that there was a chance that he wouldn't be in the bar the following night because of the outrageous hours that they were making him work. I walked to my hotel which wasn't very far, grinning at how the night worked out.

I entered the hotel and saw that the young lady wasn't behind the desk. In fact nobody was. I went up to the counter and pressed down on a bell, something I don't feel comfortable doing. I don't know why but I had a feeling if I didn't, I would be standing in the foyer for a long time. A young man appeared. He almost stopped in his tracks on seeing me and stood staring in my direction with a puzzled expression on his face but this was only momentarily before going into a routine of smiling. I showed him my receipt and a card having my room number. He gave me the key and we exchanged goodnights. After working out the system of how to open the door with the plastic card that was the key, I entered the room, feeling satisfied and having a cosy feeling. I wanted a drink of water and thought about the scene earlier in the evening when going through a series of questions with the young girl down in the foyer, one of them being if it was okay to drink the water from the tap in the bathroom and then the young man was brought into a debate that made no sense and I was none the wiser after we finished smiling and nodding at one another. Figuring it must be safe to do so, I ran the tap and used the small plastic glass that is provided to be used when brushing one's teeth. I crept into bed after a very brief time of going through the television channels. I thought of the people I had met that night in the little locals bar. They were good people. I leant out of the bed and grabbed my trousers that were slung over a chair. I pulled the brass badge from one of the pockets and ran my finger over the engraved letters, J.G.S. I smiled as I thought about the scene in the bar. I thought of the monk with the blue contact lenses and the smile on the wrestler's face. I put the badge back in the pocket and tossed the trousers over the chair. I then lay back down, looking up at the ceiling and thought about the small room that I was in and how it is just one little burrow in the honeycomb-like building that I was in and I thought about all the cavities and tunnels and the mass of convoluted, conjoined constructions making up the living-like structure of a city, that city, Kyoto and other cities. The cities are also intermeshed in a system of collaborative connections and then to other countries and then the whole planet, revolving around space, a bristling network of a cellular pattern constructed by labourers and it's fused and linked and then it can break down and be torn apart and people kill one another and then rebuild and the pattern emerges once more and the planet keeps on moving, round and round, tilting at an angle, moving at a speed that makes the bullet train seem as significant as a broken and discarded button in one of the shopping kingdoms that I had walked through that evening.

My thoughts came more down to earth as I pondered the amount of space that is taken up by a person in Japan, meaning living space in comparison to, say, a middle class American. Generally, the living space in Japan is smaller than people are accustomed to in the West unless you live in cardboard box. Then life is grim and it doesn't matter where you lay your weary cardinal piece. I looked at my room. I liked it. It was small. So what? This is Japan. I expected it to be small. It was reasonably priced, cheap when compared to similar places in Britain and after all, Kyoto is a major city. I had en-suite room, the bathroom, all of it, everything, was made of a plastic material which I was told is washed down as a whole. There is no wiping of shelves, then the walls and mopping the floor. No, the whole thing is hosed down, all in one. It's not a very interesting thing to talk about and I don't really understand what I was told about it and worse still, it gives you an insight into some of the inane things that I end up talking about to people in pubs, buses and trains.

I tried the radio and smiled at the incomprehensibility that emitted from every station. I had vague thoughts of maybe getting the World Service and a very English voice would suddenly announce itself and a sobriety would then still the small room that I was in. But there were no sedate voices speaking in my mother tongue and I turned the radio off and settled back, again going over the events in the bar. I thought of the reasons why people travel and I thought about the different tourist attractions and the things that the visitor to that isle would be interested in and commonly seek out; like traditional architecture, sacred buildings and places associated with religion and other belief systems, the difference in food, the customs like the onsens and all the other things, all the wonders and things to do that would be highlighted on the travellers itinerary and of course, not forgetting that brooding old bugger Fuji-san, being all distant but central, aloof and imbedded, Mr Grounded himself. 'Fuji,' I thought of the word and then of the people in the bar that night. That has always been the greatest interest to me. It is when being with people that I have my most enjoyment. It might be just a little bar down a little side street yet it is within the ordinariness of it all where people like me find what they are looking for. I felt good. It was a peaceful feeling as I rested with the warmth given by the people in the bar tonight and I began to fall, ebbing away from consciousness into sleep with a sound that was like an elastic band twanging and the whining pitch of voices and an interspersed collage of faces and the other sights that I had seen that day running on the cinema screen in my mind.

I'm not an early riser by nature and as I hadn't a time to vacate the room, I slumbered around the following morning, amusing myself with the television. I watched the frenetic bodily movements of the young television presenters who have a constant smile and look like they are going to fall onto the floor in raptures of laughter, seemingly at anything that was said or maybe, I thought, there are some incredibly funny people in Japan and there is a humour that simply doesn't exist in the West. I looked at the hairstyles of the presenters. At that time there was a fashion for dying hair a multitude of colours and the clothes were the same as the presenters of television shows in the West. The contestants also behaved as if the studio had been sprayed with some kind of laughing gas that causes hysterical outbursts and spasmodic bodily movements. I have noticed in recent years that back home, presenters on television shows act in a way that all of life is a party. It has come from across the Atlantic obviously and the young women presenters now open their mouths at any opportunity. I mean really opening their mouths and revealing their bleached teeth as never before and then laughing a dry hollow laugh, almost barking it out. It is aggressive and it isn't feminine. That's what I've been told and I agree. So, the culture of presentation on the television can be seen as becoming more alike with the West and Japan, meaning that there is a near frenzied manner that is also compliant to anything that comes onto the programmes. All smiles without critique as the products are farmed out through the show and the audience members sound like audience members sounded in the United States of America when I was a child.

I turned off the television and went in search of a shop that sold comforting pastries, preferably apple with icing, armed with my phrase book and a map of Kyoto. Kyoto is full of temples and shrines. These building represent, what I can gather, the major and official religions of that country which is Buddhism; the temple goers and Shintoism having the Shrines. These places are buildings or little constructions where worship is made, where devotees of that particular brand of belief or whatever you want to call it, go in order for their spiritual, philosophical, theoretical, theological, emotional and any other concerns and needs to be met. Whilst being in Japan the previous year I was interested in visiting temples with hopes of maybe trying to get a bit of knowledge in my mainly derelict mind about Buddhist thinking. Who knows, it couldn't do any harm. I went to some that were small and can be found in out of the way places or by the side of a road as was the case when I was staying down in the Izso peninsular. They all seemed to be the same, having the little rows of ash left by burning incense, the candles, a gong, little archways, quietness and a peace. There is a wooden, musty and damp smell, leafy with hardly anyone about and the colours are red. You know, 'red', the colour of Manchester United football club's strip or AC Milan's or McDonald's.

I am not aligned to any political or religious party. Those at the top of the organisation would inevitably get on my nerves. It is the common way for humans to have the propensity for creeping around the leadership, presenting a phoney pretence and deal in deceit. For me it all goes wrong when I see through their fake persona. Maybe, it's the best we have, meaning that this organised religion thing is the consummate peak of our progress. And wherever one might roam, one will find this practice in operation in one form or another. It all seems to amount to the same thing and all the factions often disagree and see their way as having the answer.

The Buddhist temples in Kyoto, from what I saw, are sold as a major tourist attraction, red and white in colour and seemed to fit in with the commercial culture. I had a little smile to myself as I pondered the symbolic links that are made when discussing religion and consumerism. The shopping malls, supermarkets and the like have been built with an uncanny resemblance to a church like structure in the UK and what with the arguments there was over Sunday opening, it can indeed be seen that to shop is to pray at the holy alter of the checkout where a monetary confession takes place. But in Japan they have built their churches that look like mass commercial concerns. Mind, I don't mean to be disrespectful in my ponderings.

Back to the temples. The buildings themselves have no historical depth in time as say, the churches in Great Britain because the vast majority of them don't go back that long. I'm not completely sure but a couple of hundred years, something like that. They are made of wood so therefore fire and earthquakes expose their fragility but also I felt it all fitted with the understanding of transience. It is in Japanese thinking to utilise what is necessary at a particular time in order to get by. Change is so much a part of the philosophy underpinning the Japanese way of adaptation in order to survive. Yet, there might be a problem for a traditionalist. That may sound contradictory considering the acceptance of a constant flux of change where the series of changes make the whole and the endless evolutionary flow of movement becomes the omnipresent way and very Buddhist it is as well in its thinking. But despite all that, there are murmurs of concern from the Buddhist world. The pervasive influences of religion has for Western observers, often been seen as the linchpin in securing social cohesion and of instilling societal responsibility and respect within and for its citizens in Japan. That is now seen by many in Japan as changing. There is the acceptance of change of course, because it is the way of things but the manner in which Japan's dominant religion is often presented and the behaviour of monks and priests of overtly brandishing material objects, along with their seeming concurrence with the socio-economic changes, it is seen as not just another variant in the movement of the flow of the water but shifting to an entirely new river where the flow will swell against a different terrain.

I walked around a few of the temples, some of the large ones and very impressive they were too. There was a library in one of them and whilst browsing in there, I thought that I saw the monk who was in Master Fuji's bar the previous night. I couldn't be sure if it was him and he wasn't wearing blue contact lenses. I said hello to the monk all the same but I didn't go down the road of asking him if he was in a bar last night wearing blue contact lenses and drinking with a group of Girl Guides from Tokyo who were in their late fifties. It could have been an uncomfortable scene. The library was an interesting place and there was a lot of literature written in English. I bought a couple of pamphlets and sat down to have a read. One article that I read was about concerns of the way Japanese society is going and the role of Buddhist religion. It told of how the lay person and also monks have become selective in what they want their faith to be and of how it is personalised and flexible to fit in around secular activities. The article gave warnings to the future of Japanese society and reiterated that well known Buddhist philosophy that all things are interdependent and that there will be harmful consequences if there is a continuance of the fragmentation of society and a lack of respect given to all its constituent parts. Indeed, I pondered. I felt the temple to be a place of importance, more than I had cynically thought a short while earlier when seeing it as little more than a tourist attraction and just another thing for the school children to tick off on a list of things Japanese. It is a place of knowledge and prophecy, offering teaching that can lead to gaining wisdom. I reflected upon on this and felt a sense of humbleness fill my insides in a warm way.

As I was walking around the temple, a young lad of about eleven years of age I would say, approached me. He was saying something in an embarrassed giggling state. I didn't have a clue what was he was going on about, so being in doubt I raised my thumb in the 'all the best' gesture. One of his friends who was holding a camera joined him. It turned out that they wanted their photograph taken with me. Now, I've a shaved head and I'm portly so they certainly didn't think that I was Mr B himself having a leisurely stroll around one of the holy places – did they? The two lads stood next to me with me puffing out my chest. This made the boys laugh and then a group of them wanted their photograph taken with me. Why? All the same, I played up, of course, aping antics of a wrestler. I don't know if I can really explain why I went through that routine. The boys liked it. The boys? What was I doing? And why did they want their photograph taken with me? And as well as that, trust my luck, there wasn't a bunch of nubile, attractive Japanese young women wanting their photograph taken with me. Oh no, no, that's not for Jumbo. For him, it's a bunch of eleven year old boys, all giggling and pulling faces.

After bidding farewell to what were most probably the bottom of the class loafers, they ambled off holding their school project papers; the subject was probably about Buddhism and they would probably get low marks but all that wouldn't bother the boys that were at school for having larks with their mates and a good time is deemed to be higher on the list of priorities than forcing oneself to try an do as the swots do who were dull and seemed to have no fun at all. And so it goes, the world over, for I was one the bottom of the class boys, seeking fun as the most important part of school life and just to be with my mates. I looked over my shoulder and watched them walk away, pushing at one another, the joker pulling a variety of facial expressions, the odd playful kick and punch being thrown, fingers pointing at new attractions that distract from what they're meant to be doing, their project papers all creased and grubby, held carelessly in hands hanging by their sides. Close by them are other pupils from the same school having the same uniform of an English naval serviceman from the Victorian era but these pupils are walking in an orderly manner. They laugh politely, their project papers neatly in place on a clip board, with a pen in one hand, stopping at points of interest to make notes and cross reference information already noted.

The temples are good places to visit and although there are people meditating and praying, I didn't find a little bit of space where one can be by oneself in quietude. As I've said, they were very touristy. The particular temple that I was walking about in was massive, made of wood, great trunks bound together, having large wooden walkways and different halls with impressive flooring. Everything made of timber. It was wood, wood, wood and I thought of a piece of Buddhist thinking that I had come across - 'This isn't living – just a preparation for the next life'. You try telling that to the trees that were used in building the temple.

I left the temple and wandered around the city having a look at what I thought were interesting places, just places that caught my eye and of course stopping in the shops selling pastries to portly outsiders who have a sweet tooth. I sampled the different forms of transport and what I noticed on more than one occasion was how people shoed frustration at just missing a bus or train. There was no cursing or shaking a fist, kicking the side of the train, threatening the driver with all methods of gore and damning his mother to hell, no glaring at a passer-by who dares to catch the eye of the person has had the train doors close in his or maybe her face. It was meek or that's how I saw it in that snapshot view. I felt it to be an odd response when running for a train and just missing it, to offer an embarrassed smile at one's foolish' predicament. I saw a man just step backwards when the bus doors closed just as he reached it. Showing no outward expression, he looked in a way that he hoped his mistake hadn't bothered anyone.

I went back to the hotel for a rest before going out in the evening. The young woman from the previous day was behind the reception desk. She looked at me and smiled but I could detect that under her mandatory smile resided an apprehension that she was going to be engaged in some confusing dialogue. But it didn't happen. I smiled and nodded, walked into the lift and went to my room. I tried the radio just to see if there was a familiar voice and then I settled to hearing any other language, like German, French or Spanish coming from the speaker but it wasn't to be. The television had lots of news programmes and shows that had young people presenting them from behind a large desk. Fast camera direction showed close ups of faces contorted in hysterics and the eye of the camera cut at all angles and across the studio, shepherded by waves of laughter and the faces flashed on the screen and the audience clapped and adverts interjected the frenzy which at first I thought were part of the show. I lay back and let my thoughts unravel. I was sure that Japan had changed from my last visit which was only the previous year. My thoughts wrestled between the way that Japanese culture acquiesces and accommodates. I was sure that in the previous year, I didn't see the amount of 'hip hop' type of fashion about, with the gangster rap style of dress and manner. I'm sure that it was more evident on my second trip. But is it just the way that Japan copies the West and even if the Western way has the big say, is it only fashion? When the young men or women take off their baseball hats, does he or she also discard Yankee Joe? Maybe it's just superficial to them and what is more meaningful is the importance of ancestral heritage. Is that really at the front of a young Japanese mind? Trust and respect, group values and a network of relationships that keep the machine running smoothly?

I wonder. The wants and needs of others. It doesn't seem to be the resonating tune being played on all channels in the West or anywhere else for that matter – and India and China are rising. There seems to be a deference given to systems in Japan and although that exists in other societies, in Japan individuals across the board appear to show respect and duty to the powers that be or at least don't make a public show of ridiculing or lambasting them.

I thought it strange when I cracked my jokes, calling McDonald's McKhuso's because the Japanese word for 'shit' sounds like 'khuso'. It was met with embarrassed giggles as if being so disrespectful to a dominant institution. Is Consumerism the New Religion? I don't think so although a lot of people think it is or might be. But places like Japan are consumer crazy anyway. Shops and shopping plays a bigger part in that culture than the one that I come from even though that might be hard believe when one sees major roads in North London blocked with traffic carrying people to buy a piece of furniture that looks like any other piece of furniture but it has to be bought from a particular store where it is fashionable to do so. It is not the practice of shopping in the new religion that marks a distinct difference from what has gone on before but the incredibly shrinking number of companies or corporations that drive the global wheel of fortune. This can be argued as being the principal factor in the new development as fewer companies own more and more and they are growing in power and influence. Faith to dominance? Having faith in corporations? The massive corporations seem to fragment a society. I thought of Riki Shi gladly accepting his cheque from a representative of a huge company and nodding reverently to the paymaster that has a powerful role within the society.

Things have changed in Japan, a policy has been passed by the Japanese government that works towards dismantling employment practices where there is a security of employment and shrugging off the custom that had a concept of reciprocal loyalty as a major principle within it concerning matters of age and length of time employed by a company. This is favourable to business practices giving that much wanted flexibility for employers and especially for the opportunistic multinationals to have a malleable workforce – and Buddhist monks now drive flash cars and imbibe the objects offered by materialism. The monks are exhibiting selectivity in their approach to their religion because it is a choice ridden system – don't you know.

I closed my eyes and listened to that hum one hears in hotels, the feeling of being in a vacuum began to fill my senses and I wafted into a place where sleep takes the travelling unlikely fooligans of this world.

It was early evening. I left the hotel and went into a place for something to eat and for the first time, I pointed at a plastic re-creation of what the actual food looked like when it was assembled to make a specific meal. From there I went for a stroll around the centre of Kyoto and like the previous night, the air was full of wet drizzle but on this evening it wasn't as heavy. My ankle burned. The pain that I thought was caused by gout tightened and so I slowed my pace and even stopped at times to rest it. The flat footed fooligan!

I went into a couple of bars, choosing ones that I thought were traditional rather than the replicas of something else or part of a chain having a theme. I went into one bar that was very narrow and reminded me of a small railway carriage. I entered by sliding a door across which was more like a screen and when I turned, I saw that the bar counter was little more than an arm's length in front of me. The whole bar was this width. It was thick with smoke and loud with the noise of people engaged in banter. The bar was in a little alleyway, cramped alongside other businesses. It was claustrophobic and having an intense ambience charged with activity – and I liked it.

A group of young men entered, full of good humour and high spirits. I tried to make room but there wasn't any yet this didn't deter them or bother any other of the patrons. They worked their way to the other end of the bar and then one of them looked at me and shouted, 'Beckham!' I made the gesture that I had before, the mock rejection and pushing my hand away. The young man shouted, saying no and he wagged his finger at me for responding in such a manner when the hallowed one's name was brought up. He and a couple of his friends tried to engage conversation but it was futile. It was too cramped to pull out my phrase book and it needed more than that to join in with some bar chat. They reeled out a few English football teams, wanting to know what one I supported. I had gathered that. "Fulham," I said proudly, knowing the reaction that it would get. Confused looks were exchanged between the young men. Although not long after this time, a Japanese footballer started playing at Fulham and if that had of been the case at this time, they would surely have heard of Fulham Football Club, SW6. They were a pleasant bunch and we raised glasses at each other.

I watched the two young men behind the counter taking the little skewers of meat, cooking them and preparing vegetables, taking the cigarettes from their mouths to perform an action that demanded two hands. I smiled as I thought of health and safety laws, hygiene standards and the lack of food poisoning that people get in Japan when eating in restaurants and bars. I left the cramped drinking establishment and walked around that part of Kyoto before making my way back to the area where the hotel was and walking down the side streets towards Master Fuji's bar. I was beginning to familiarise myself with the district. I slid open the door and there I was, back in the world of Master Fuji. It had a buzz. There was a different crowd from the previous night. The wrestler wasn't there and I was disappointed to see that the tall Malayan man also wasn't in the bar. Master Fuji came over and shook my hand. We engaged in a bit of a conversation that was within the limits permitted by limited language. The young man was behind the bar. He raised a knife, nodded and smiled. Master Fuji explained that the Malayan man wasn't going to be in the bar that night and he pointed to the space at the bar occupied by the patient translator last night. It was a shame because communication was difficult and also I would have liked to have said goodbye and good luck to him. I thought him to be one of the good people one bumps into in life. A short while later, as I was coming out of the toilet, I realised that Master Fuji was shouting at me, "Jumbo, Jumbo," he said and in an animated way as he pointed at the telephone that he was holding. It took a second to sink in that it was for me. It was the Malayan man, ringing from work. He offered his apologies as he had to work till after midnight and wouldn't be able to come down for a drink. I wished him all the best and after another beer, I called it a night. Master Fuji came from behind the bar and stood with me on the pavement outside, shaking my hand and telling me something. It seemed serious and we said our goodbyes. It's a very big misfortune for humans, this problem that we have with communication. I walked though the narrow streets, thinking of the lives of the people that slumbered in the little houses around me.

* * * * * * * *

The next morning I packed my bags and pulled my case to the station. I stopped at the tourist office to see a woman who worked there. I had spoken to her the day before. She spoke some English and I had arranged to pick up some posters of trains for my nephew. She told me that she had to get them from the back and went off to get them. The posters were neatly rolled into a tube and as she handed them to me, I felt that she gave me a look in a way that a doctor might study a patient when I went into a bit of my slapstick routine. We wished each other good luck and after trying to find a place in the side of my case for the posters, I went to the station. The first thing that I wanted to do when getting into the station was ring Jon, my friend in central Tokyo who I had planned to stay with; the one who works in banking who I had stayed with a week before. I don't know why but I was amazed, surprised and relieved when I successfully made contact with him on the telephone. He arranged to meet me outside a station in central Tokyo which is in an area that is referred to as the business district. We agreed to meet outside the same coffee house as before.

An Unlikely Fooligan

I found out what track the venerable Shinkansen was leaving from and reserved a seat. I then took a leisurely walk over to the platform and stood behind a number that is marked out on the floor denoting where the carriage having that number will stop. The journey back to Tokyo was smooth. I was in a languid and dreamy state, dozing off, watching the red light move along the map. I bought my nephew a souvenir from a vending machine on the train. It was a key ring with a picture of a bullet train on the fob. It looked like something from the late 1960's.

Nine

I left the bullet train in Tokyo and went from being in a state of slumber and relaxation to entering a frenzied web of confusion as I searched for the subway train that would take me the few stops to where I was going. I found the train and managed to alight at the correct station, walked to where I had planned to meet my friend and there he was. I had a few days left of my holiday and they were to be spent in Tokyo.

My friend's flat was hi-tech and being on the twenty forth floor, it gave fantastic views across Tokyo. At night, when coming in, I stood and looked out on the neon lights, twinkling and flashing, an all-absorbing intensity as the buildings turned into nocturnal mountains that sparkled. On entering the kitchen and opening the refrigerator, a voice in a metallic American sounding accent would say, "Hi" and greet the occupant by his Christian name. My friend was amused by the toilet that was laden with gadgets. Mind, it didn't speak to you whilst using it which I was glad about because being spoken to with some else's name whilst on the throne could be disconcerting. In the evening I was taken to the haunts used by the expatriate business workers, some of those I spoke to had never been into the type of bar that I sought out even though having lived or stayed in Japan for years. During the course of one evening, I was told by one English city chap who was working in Japan that I was, 'Bangers and mash' and even 'Old school'. I think that he was alluding to my values, seeing them as basic and not being impressed by the posturing in clubs – something like that. I might be 'out of the loop' but what place does the 'loop' want to be? And I'm often seen as being an uncompromising sort of person but remember, I am also a Japanese Girl Guide and I wore my badge with pride – for I endeavour to do my best and try to help others when I can, as I meet them, just like the good people in Master Fuji's bar had done so.

I found the corporate playgrounds – meaning the lounges, bars, disco clubs or whatever – to be unimaginative. I saw business students wearing the beads and trinkets taken from world culture, only the third world price has been omitted as it has now been designed and packaged to the new world consumer. There are those who have constructed places that are an emulation of what exists in the UK with the threat and edge taken out. It's no different to the old days and ways of the empire I suppose whether it's Raffles created by the 'old school' business venture or its new version Ragamuffins, brimming with a fashion styled on liberal democracy. I went into a few of these designer establishments where they play wallpaper music having an Antipodean mix with an American twang and fused with a fake London Town accent and also drizzle a little South African flavour to create the outdoor beat, all inspired by marketing boards – the dress, style and language is peppered with hedonism and a high regard for economic practices that create profit and furnish territories to be exploited by the 'chill out', credit card ravers who dance to the spiritual heart beat that is laid down by the church of the World Bank. Not everybody was a city dealer type. There were the travelling gap year students, reading their choice of beverage from a menu, literally, that was as native to Japan as KFC. "Travel broadens the mind," I thought to myself. Six thousand miles from home and the adventuring spirit is a risky business as it's practiced in a room that is safe and familiar where the stage has been erected and the script and props are ready. All one has to do is turn up. And old 'bangers and mash' had a look at the 'dressing down' culture. Although working in an office environment, you would think that they snowboard to work by the way a lot of them talk. "Hey, he abseiled into the office window this morning," and everyone is paragliding, bungee jumping, parachuting, hiking, biking, trekking, camping, sledging, canoeing, horse riding into the sea or camel riding across the dunes and maybe even astral jumping – give me a pogo stick!

I had a chat with a couple of people belonging to the business community. At this time, the West's invasion into Iraq was imminent and one of these people was telling me about the slump in shares but there were good times coming because things had been prepared and as soon as the bombs start dropping, the shares would start rising. I went into free fall thinking, the feel of people having a desire for people to be killed in Iraq so that the index rises, the boom, boom, blah, blah of fatuous popular music, the constructed creations embedded in the social life of people who perform predictable fashionable actions where the body language follows a pre-determined code – and I yearned to be in a place away from all of it.

My friend who put me up couldn't have been more obliging. He gave me a spare key so that I could come and go at my leisure and so during the days, I would saunter my way around Tokyo and in the evenings we went for a drink. Very enjoyable it was. I bought myself a train pass for the day and armed with a map and my phrase book, wandered off. One afternoon whilst on a train I watched a young man as he read one of the thick Manga comics. I'm not sure what the content was that he was reading but the youth appeared to be engrossed as his look penetrated through the thick lenses of his glasses and fixed onto the roughly cut pulp paper of the magazine. The Manga comic is a very popular item, so much so it is synonymous with Japan. They are read by all age groups and are classified and categorised for their suitability relating to gender and age. There is a penchant for giving graphic images and descriptions of sex and violence. Manga is the Japanese word for comics. I took a closer look at the pages of the comic that he was holding and then I looked at his face. He was grinning, looking near imbecilic, a film of sweat coating his spotty face and he raised his head, nearly gratefully from the thick book with its roughly cut pages showing simply sketched cartoons of school girls in distress. The light in the train carriage caught in the lenses of the youth's glasses and his mouth rounded tremulously as his eyes nearly closed at his sensual thoughts.

I thought about this area of Japanese culture that has been widely discussed. The attitude towards sex has many complexities and apparent contradictions. I thought about how spotty youths and greasy men leer at cartoon drawings of young girls in public and then look away from the comic to stare at a giggling girl standing with her friends, all adorned in designer things and Mr Greasy Face ponders possibilities of getting his shaking mitts on the young flesh as he considers how much money he will shell out for a bag or a phone.

The train emerged from being underground and I looked out of the window at the rain as it pelted against the window. The Tokyo urban sprawl was grey and dull, wet concrete, cramped, utilitarian, a post war, post earthquake human habitat. There is no excess. That is only reflected in the price for certain goods and certain notions that aspire to a time and people that seems distant in this claustrophobic rush that exists in prefabricated concrete that is moulded into box shapes and people enter and leave the carriage, their bodies altering as they meet the different elements. I look at a rain sodden man, unctuous in his ways as he eyes potential excitement within the carriage, maybe whiskey dissipating his inhibitions and maybe today he will do it, place his hand on her body, lean in closer than normal and a deep tiredness drains through his body and his mind numbs as the warmth in the train feels heavy and he thinks of the obligations and responsibilities he has, his boss and family. He looks over, the ringing sound that rises from a group of school girls, tugging at their thick white socks, adjusting the waist bands of their dresses, the lucky charms tied to their mobile phones are fingered absently. The thought strikes him maybe, that they are childlike but he moves closer, positioning himself behind one of the stragglers and maybe the girl senses him and her unmarked skin flushes and he thinks of the disgrace to himself and his family so he backs off because everything would be ruined. His mind is racing, fevered with the drive of alcohol and frustration and he moves away giving just the briefest of looks back at what torments him and he curses the constrictions in his life. He steps from the train as the doors open to the wind and rain that in a way wake him to the drudgery and guilt that he feels filling his life.

I also stepped off the train at the next station and I walked around the streets that were somewhere in the Tokyo area, walking past and along narrow streets, some not wide enough for a small car to drive down. Pink flowers, blossom I suppose, battled in their soft way to remain intact, to hold their shape and offer a natural colour as the rain swept down upon them. I looked up at the balconies and at the pushbikes and the crowded mass of signs advertising businesses, the faces of older people staring at me and I stopped at a vending machine and bought my favourite drink, a can of Procari Sweat. It is an acquired taste, a carbonated drink that is meant to have health giving properties like nutrients and electrolytes, belonging to the growing group of what are referred to as 'sports drinks'. A ringing and clanging sound drew my attention. It was a place where people go inside and play pachinko. They are known as Pachinko Parlours. I walked inside and immediately drew the attention of a moody looking bloke who let smoke drift out from his lips slowly so that it formed a plume over his face. His eyes were set deep in a face that had dents and scars impressed into its skin. He wasn't going to look away from me until he was ready to do so. The loud clatter was deafening. I walked around, not knowing what I was looking at. Rows and rows of the tall machines were being worked tirelessly as production machines in an industrial workshop. Pachinko is big business. I have read that it employs more people in Japan than the steel industry and makes up to forty per cent of Japan's leisure industry. Mainly those having Korean origin run the business and it's inextricably bound to the criminal culture. The people playing the game stood zombie-like in front of the vertical pinball machines, their bodies amidst clouds of cigarette smoke and the deafening sound as the steel ball bearings tumble down the machines. Eyes gaze at the seemingly infinite waves of what looks like spherical steel ants that rebound, ricochet and shuffle for placement as if each one of the ball bearings has a mind of its own. I found it difficult to breathe because of the smoke and the hard sounding racket grated so much that it was uncomfortable. I left the building under the gaze of Mr Moody, a man who looked about as healthy and wholesome as an infected wound. The light rain was a pleasant reception and even the polluted air felt fresh to my senses as I stepped outside.

* * * * * * * * *

The weather was far more clement the following day. Armed with my phrase book and a couple of maps I went on my micro-nomadic saunter around Tokyo whilst my friend was at work in the bank contributing to shaping the means that dictate the way that we live our lives. But nothing so heavy was on the day's agenda for this portly traveller. My mission involved finding a good pastry shop whilst wandering amongst the inhabitants of the great city that is both turbulent and yet composed as it goes about its way of simmering though another day. I stood in a carriage of a train, absorbing the rays of sun coming through the window. My mood was serene and content. I noticed a man in a suit holding a briefcase. He was looking at me and when I looked at him, he looked away and adjusted his glasses on his nose. He reminded me of a man the previous year who gently tapped me on my arm when I was on a crowded train. When I turned he nearly stood to attention as he asked ...

"Excuse me sir, are you fooligan, sir?"
"Yes, yes I am," I said, with no change of expression.
"Ah, thank you sir," he said and he bowed just a little as he backed off.

Fooligan, Beckham and even Bruce Willis. These are names that would stay with me along with the manner of the Japanese people. I was warned about one particular trait by my friend who lived in Isehara. It is to do with the Japanese sense of obligation, duty, loyalty or whatever one wants to call it. He told me to be careful about asking directions because there are some people who will go to extreme measures in order to fulfil what they believe to be an obligation. He told me a story about an incident that happened to him many years before when he approached a man who was in his car with his wife. He asked how to get to a place which was miles away and it really was miles away. It took the man hours to drive there with my friend sitting in the back of the car embarrassed as hell because this civic minded chap had taken it upon himself to drive him to where he wanted to go – it took hours. The man was in a bad mood. It was many, many miles out of his way and he snapped at his wife, cursing the situation he was in. He ignored pleas from my friend who told the man to stop and that he would be able to get to the place by himself. In the end, my friend gave up and just sat there in the back of the car with the man going on about the way that his day had gone. The man had carried out what he saw as a responsibility. I experienced this commitment for myself that afternoon although only minor in comparison but during the course of it, I was reminded of what my friend had told me. I was in the centre of the city looking for a street. I had a map but was having difficulty working out where the street was. Some of the older inhabitants can give you a dismissive look as you approach them so it's best to try the younger people. Some of them like to try out their English. I approached a young couple that were standing by the side of a busy intersection waiting for the lights to change. The man was standing there in a white shirt and trousers with his arms by his side whilst the woman with him was holding a young baby in her arms. She was dressed in a rather tight fitting dress and shoes having a heel on them. It looked like they had been to a formal occasion of some kind. I asked the man if he could help me showing him the map and pointing to the street that I wanted. It was written in English and Japanese. The young man pointed diagonally across the road junction and then saying something, made a pecking gesture with his hand which I took as meaning that I had to carry on walking for quite a bit further down the road I needed to take. It became confusing and I saw that the young man was becoming frustrated because what he was trying to communicate was essentially a simple piece of information. He wasn't irritated but rather upset that he wasn't making himself understood. He then moved quickly, gesturing for me to follow him. Walking to another part of the intersection, talking to me over his shoulder as he walked at quite a pace. I looked round and saw that the woman was following but finding it difficult to keep up, what with her dress, the shoes and the small matter of having a baby in her arms which she juggled against herself to gain a greater hold. I tried to tell the young man that it was okay and that I knew the direction where to go but it was hopeless. He was a man on a mission and he didn't seem to be bothered about his wife; that's who I took her to be as she struggled along behind us. Every time I turned and asked if she was okay, she would smile and nod and even attempt a slight bow of her head whilst she laboured along with the baby in her arms. And it was hot, very hot in fact and humid.

We had crossed the intersection and then waited for the lights to change so that we could cross another road and just as the woman caught up, the lights changed and the young man was off, looking at me over his shoulder, pushing forward, smiling, speaking. I was feeling guilty about the woman and I kept turning to see if she was okay. She would nod, smile and nod some more. I looked at the baby jiggling in her arms and the look on the young woman's face seemed to be apologetic for being such a hindrance. And the young man kept walking. We crossed two more main roads. There he was, looking over his shoulder, one hand raised, doing the pecking gesture and I looked back at the woman. I was between the two of them. "What have I done?" I thought to myself. I've intruded upon their afternoon causing this disruption but the young woman maintained her pleasant manner. I noticed that the baby was wearing a hat. It was a thick woollen hat having small ears sown on the sides but quite high up, much higher than where the ears would be. They looked a bit like Mickey Mouse ears. And still we carried on. And then the young man stopped and stood on the corner of a road, nearly laughing, pointing to a road; the one I wanted. I shook his hand and he nodded continually, smiling at what had been such a laugh, the sweat running down the side of his face; and then the young woman joined us. She was sweating but also nearly laughing at the crazy fun we were having. I kept apologising for causing such an inconvenience but they wouldn't hear of it. I looked at the baby in the young woman's arms. He was awake, what else? A nice little chap he was and those ears made him more endearing although I thought it way too hot to be wearing a thick woollen bonnet. I touched the baby's cheek and the happy parents smiled and I then went into a short slapstick routine, puffing out my stomach and chest, pulling a face and pointing at the baby. This caused an immediate outburst of laughter from the proud parents and I tweaked the ears on the hat. The young man took the baby from the woman and handed him to me. I must say he seemed a content little fellow, what with the assault course experience he had just been through. I jiggled the baby gently, pulling a face and then the young woman took a camera from her jacket pocket. "I didn't reckon for this," was my thought as I stood on the busy pavement having my photo taken holding young Master Tokyo dressed in his silly bloody hat. And then the young man stopped a passer by, an unsuspecting man in a suit and asked him if he would take a photograph of the four of us, mum, dad, baby and that lump the foreigner. The young couple seemed exceptionally pleased with the attention I gave their baby. It was a pleasure meeting them as it was with the other people I bumped into during my two trips in TLOTRS.

There are the swanky areas to visit in Tokyo which I walked through but it didn't mean much to me. I mean, expensive shops and restaurants aren't my thing and probably never would be even if I won the lottery. On one of the final days of my trip, I followed the directions on my map to the Transportation Museum which wasn't in the ritzy area. Nearby to the museum were small shops selling model trains and planes, second hand transformers and other gadgets. I had slipped into the world of the Japanese 'anorak' and I took my place amongst them, looking at a model of a Shinkansen train. I felt a fraud because I know nothing of electronic gadgetry. I have romantic notions about the bullet train but I have no knowledge of engineering and I have no interest in being a member of a model railway club or standing for hours near an airport with high powered binoculars and then writing furiously in a note book when sighting something deemed significant. I am not criticising the people involved in these pursuits in any way and in fact, it would be a far better place if people had an interest rather than be a dumb receptor and follow the cyclical replication of fickle demands. I was standing with men and it was only men, in cramped shops. I watched them study minute miniature replicas of say, a park bench or a spanner that a railway worker the size of one's fingernail will be holding. There were furrowed brows as electronic bits and pieces were examined. Deference was shown by standing with one's hands behind one's back, looking on attentively as a piece of kit was being shown to another customer. I was in a world of men having obsessive interests that are played out, often in solitary conditions. Look, I'm no fashion authority on the style of clothing and I don't care what people wear but I noticed, as I have noticed before in my life, that there is a definite style of dress being a preferred style of presentation that demarcates the studiously driven model engineer from others in society. I noted the singular taste in putting together the clothes, not a single designer item amongst them. The fashion fascist overlords would be biting their hands at the sight of it. A chap who I would guess was in his late sixties spoke to me, telling me that he had been to England, Wales and Scotland, travelling on the trains but it was very difficult to understand what he was saying. The best I could offer in return was to keep repeating 'Shinkansen' and giving him the thumbs up sign. But I did feel a fraud, not a sneak but a fraud. I had entered their world and stood alongside them without having the interests that they have.

The transport museum was very well organised as one would expect. On the top floor of the museum was an assortment of exhibitions pertaining to the history of the Japanese aeronautical industry. There were films and videos, parts of planes and information on military and civil aeroplanes. Japanese Airlines were well represented showing many photographs of the early passenger planes, the people who worked on them and the passengers themselves. I found it very interesting and the quality of its presentation was excellent as were the trains in the lower part of the museum.

The train section took up by far the largest part of the transport museum. It was a schoolboy's heaven and for adults it was also the building of bliss. There were demonstrations, all watched heedfully and respectfully by eleven year old boys standing alongside grown men whose ages spanned over generations and most standing in that pose with hands behind backs. There were simulators of different types of trains, the bullet train simulator being the jewel in the crown. I watched a young boy carefully start the great machine's energy and drive it out of a station, high tech graphics played on a screen in front. The boy was flanked by two men who watched over the proceedings with serious intent. One had to have a considerable amount of knowledge in order to drive the venerable bullet train. I stood in the cab and looked across the massive dashboard. I know it's not called that but that's the limit to my knowledge. I looked through the window over the extensive nose. What an invention! I tried my skill at slowing down a train and stopping it at a platform in a station. It was a simulator of what is called a local train. In comparison to the bullet train the interior was vastly different in that it was basic, there being a couple of metal handles, a speedometer and not much else. All the same, there wouldn't be many Japanese commuters pushing at one another to get on the train if I was driving. It took great skill to stop the train at the correct place and I didn't have it. As I was in the simulator of a local train, I thought about the drivers that I had stood behind, looking at the advancing station over their shoulders, their hands in pristine white cotton gloves on the handles just like the ones I was holding. I thought what those drivers must have thought, having Mr Portly, the middle-aged foreigner looking over their shoulder whilst they were negotiating the signals and watching their speed.

I liked the museum. It must induce a hundred fantasies a day in the minds of young boys who visit the place. At least there was no killing, shooting, slaying and blowing up, the kind of thing that exists in pastimes that have been created by adults for a child's imagination to be let loose whilst playing computer games. Yes, it gave me a warm feeling in the cynical, competing and brutal world that we are told is the normal experience in contemporary society. Here I was in a place that contested all that.

A ridiculous amusement was to follow when I saw an orderly queue of boys standing in front of a machine. I went over to investigate and discovered that they were waiting their turn to get a replica ID pass of a Shinkansen driver. One had to stand in front of a screen and have a photograph taken. After a few minutes, a laminated ID pass dropped from the machine with one's photograph on it. There was wording but all I could make out was 'Shinkansen'. After that, all one had to do was place it in a little plastic sheaf that was provided and there you are! One is an honoured Shinkansen driver and there is the ID pass to prove it! I pulled a stupid face for my photograph which wasn't hard of course. To give the reader of this account a further insight into my life in the fast lane, I still carry my photo ID pass in my wallet thus proving that I am a Shinkansen driver - so there!

****

The last few days were spent doing what I feel I do best and that is wandering around. I was getting the hang of the way of things as is often the way, just as my time was coming to an end. I was getting used to not pulling a silly face when buying something in a shop but would wait for the person to add it up on a pocket calculator and show me the total. It is something that is nearly always done. I was becoming familiar with the place as a tourist. I'm sure it would take a long time to familiarise oneself with all the complexities that exist if one was to live in Japan. There would be things I would never get used to, such as trying to fit my legs under a low table in a restaurant. The custom of taking off one's shoes and slipping on a pair of flip- flop sandals on entering the toilet is a good idea. It makes sense not to transmit germs from one place to the other. I forgot to do this again on one of my last days when being in a restaurant and going to the toilet. An elderly man lambasted me, pointing to my shoes and a heap of sandals by the door and his expression didn't alter when I offered my apologies. Innocence equalled stupidity and disrespect to this man. And good on him for he was upholding a standard that protects all of us.

I hadn't been in Japan for long but I was missing food that was soft and comforting, something like a heap of mashed potatoes or thick, warm bread and butter maybe with honey and whilst I'm about it, bread and butter pudding or jam roly poly with custard or even treacle sponge pudding. I wanted to get away from the protein driven food frenzy or even fury and although I know nothing about the reserve stock of fish in the sea, I would say it has to be threatened because fish is in abundance everywhere in Japan. It was something that made me feel a bit queasy at times. The place oozes fish as if people are sustained by aquatic matter to an extent that they are themselves fish creatures. When thinking of this, it gave me an atavistic chill down my back - to my long lost fin and scales. And here we are, living on land, at the moment at any rate, dressed in clothes and all the rest of it but we're the biggest hunter. It is to sickening proportions that we hunt, extract and use. The thought stayed in my mind of how could Master Blue Planet sustain this daily pillaging and abuse? But fish really is everywhere. Pre-packed tiny fish in cellophane pockets, in cartons, boxes, tins and all the other ways of packaging. I saw something that I thought was just seaweed but on closer inspection, I could see that amongst the green mush were tiny eyes on the end of fibre optic looking mini-creatures, all meshed together. They are sometimes sold in the area of shops where they sell confectionary products and there they are, sold in vacuum packed bags. Anyway, if I lived in Japan I would want to get away from the ever-present presence of it and gain a softer feel. Mr Bangers and Mash indeed, well, just the mash for me.